Are you crossing your fingers and
hoping that you will attain your goals?

What does your financial picture look
like today? What will that financial
picture look like in the future?

Is your money working for you?

Are you subjecting yourself and your family to
unnecessary risk?

Turn the page to discover
Planning can help you add
other critical financial issue
today...

Personal Finance

I

Acknowledgments

I must thank several wonderful people who helped me complete *Perfect Money Planning*. I particularly wish to thank Bill O'Quin for creative guidance and inspiration. A special thank you to Eddie Selover and Joan Barrett for editing this work. I wish to thank Joe Mahoney, Dave Dukehart and Bryant Kirk for their support in helping me make this book available to you.

To Stephanie my wife, thank you for your understanding and willingness to sacrifice some of our time together. Finally, I'd like to thank Carl and Rose for being wonderful parents.

Illustrations courtesy of Presentation Task Force, New Vision Technologies, Inc., and Clickart, T./Maker Company. Permission granted to modify the Kiplinger's Personal Finance Magazine retirement calculator for use in this book.

Contents

Introduction

1 The Financial Roller Coaster Ride
2 The 100 Person Story
3 Future Shock in Action
4 Get Started
4 The Six Perspectives of Financial Planning
6 Snapshots in Time

Chapter 1 - The Future And Your Finances

7 Taxes in the Future
7 The National Debt
7 Social Security
8 Nationalized Health Care
8 Tax Trends?
10 The Banking System in the Future
10 Life Expectancies Increase?
10 Unconventional Phases in Life
10 Self-Appraisal Questions

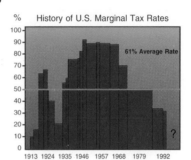

Chapter 2 - Getting Started

11 Establishing an Emergency Fund
11 Establishing a Contingency Day
11 Financial Organization
13 Determining Your Priorities
14 Setting Goals
15 Impending Changes
15 Financial Professionals
16 Personal Asset Inventory
16 Your Legal Documents

Chapter 3 - Debt Management

17 Credit Cards
18 Qualifying for Credit
18 Car Loans
19 Home Equity Loans
21 Advice for Those Drowning in Debt
21 Filing for Bankruptcy
22 Creditor-Proof Assets

Chapter 4 - Federal Taxes

23 Federal Taxes
24 Projecting Your Taxes
25 Federal Income Tax Strategies
26 Federal Transfer Tax
27 An Estate Planning Example

Chapter 5 - Insurance

29 Life Insurance and Its Tax Advantages
29 Mortality
31 Administration
31 Investment
32 Accelerated Benefits
33 A Look at the Mechanics

40 How Much Insurance Do You Need?
41 Inflation and Your Life Insurance
42 Disability Insurance Protection
42 The Question
44 Property and Casualty Insurance
45 Health Insurance
46 Long Term Care
46 Medicare
47 Insurance You May Not Need
47 Credit Card Insurance
47 Flight and Accidental Death Insurance
48 Option to Purchase Additional Insurance
48 Consumer Purchase Insurance
48 Dread-Disease Insurance
48 Student Accident Insurance

Chapter 6 - Investing For The Future
49 Understanding Risk, Holding Periods and the Erosion Effect
52 Investment Selector
52 Investment Alternatives
56 Investment Checklist
57 Dollar Cost Averaging
59 Predicting the Market Direction

Chapter 7 - Mortgage Acceleration Options
61 Mortgage Acceleration Options
62 Five Scenarios Reviewed
63 Alternative Strategies Compared

Chapter 8 - College Funding
67 The Cost of College
68 The Six Perspectives Applied
70 College Funding Summary

Chapter 9 - Retirement Planning
71 Pre-Retirement
73 The Three Legs of Retirement Income
73 Social Security
74 Employer-Sponsored Plans
75 Individual Plans
81 Post-Retirement
82 Summary

Chapter 10 - Implementing Your Financial Plan
83 Choosing a Financial Consultant
84 Compensation
85 Choosing a Financial Service Company
87 Conclusion

Appendix A - Your Financial Plan

Appendix B - The Value of $1 Compounded

Index

The secret to financial success is consistent growth. A solid plan will minimize both risk and the obstacles to your success. Today, the average family spends more time planning their two-week vacation than their retirement, which may last twenty or more years. Consequently, most people make financial decisions in a reactive manner. Planning for the future is something most people never seem to address. Keep in mind that the only person who can take care of the older person you will someday be is the younger working person you are now.

Fortunately, financial planning can be interesting and even fun. Completing the exercises in this book will allow you, in just a few hours, to start a comprehensive financial plan.

The Financial Roller Coaster Ride

Making financial decisions in a reactive manner results in a depressing financial roller coaster ride of increasing and decreasing net worth. This roller coaster ride is inevitable when you fail to plan your finances. Understanding the roller coaster effect is instrumental in achieving financial success. Consider this simple example.

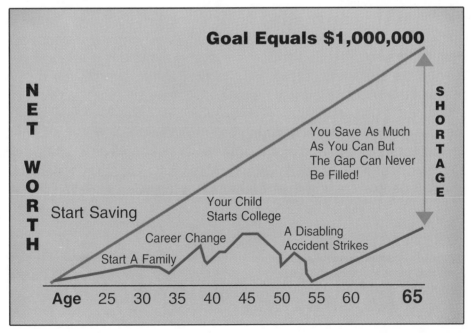

The green line represents steady growth in your net worth. The blue line represents what most people actually experience -- a roller coaster ride.

The dynamic nature of life directly affects our cash flow. You must see the "big picture" in order to avoid one of the most common reasons for financial failure -- saving to spend. Saving to spend is not necessarily a bad thing, but what we actually buy is not always consistent with our goals. Accumulating wealth on a consistent basis is one of the most important methods to achieve financial success. Few people attain financial success from stock market speculation or winning a lottery.

This mental exercise may help you better understand the power of systematic saving. Imagine for a moment that all of your assets are gathered in a pile. Now imagine removing your liabilities from your assets. How big is the remaining pile? If you are like most people, what you have accumulated is wealth due to systematic saving. Examples of systematic saving are home equity, company pension accumulation and life insurance cash values. The three examples mentioned comprise the bulk of most peoples' net worth.

Another key point often overlooked is wealth protection. Proper protection involves adequate property and casualty coverage, income replacement protection and creditor proofing your assets. Inadequate protection of your assets can forever destroy your goal of financial independence.

The 100 Person Story
The financial future does not appear to be as secure as it used to be for many Americans. There are increasing demands on employer-sponsored retirement programs. The Social Security system is under tremendous financial and demographic pressure. To make matters worse, the national savings rate is only 3% of annual income.

Many people will live in poverty during their retirement years. A recent study by the Department of Health and Human Services has highlighted the fact that few people achieve financial success during retirement. The study concluded that for every 100 people starting their careers, the following situation exists at age 65...

25 are dead
20 have annual incomes under $6,000
51 have annual incomes between $6,000 and $35,000;
   median income is $12,000
4 have annual incomes over $35,000

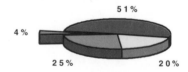

Source: U.S. Department of Health and Human Services, SSA Pub #13-11871, 6/90.

Unfortunately, a majority of people may experience poverty in their retirement years. Only four out of 100 may be financially successful. The point to be made is clear. You can achieve financial success. Planning your success is a necessity, not a luxury.

Only four out of 100 are financially successful.

Future Shock in Action

Consider the following situation in which a couple plans to retire in 20 years. How much money must be saved if they project Social Security and current pension benefits to fall short of their retirement goal by $30,000 per year? If inflation is 5% and this couple can earn 8% consistently after taxes, the fund needed to provide for retirement from age 65 to age 85 is staggering.

Current Age: 45   Inflation: 5%
Years To Retirement: 20   Net Return: 8%
Goal: $30,000 in today's dollars for twenty years at a minimum.

The future amount needed to equal $30,000 today is startling.

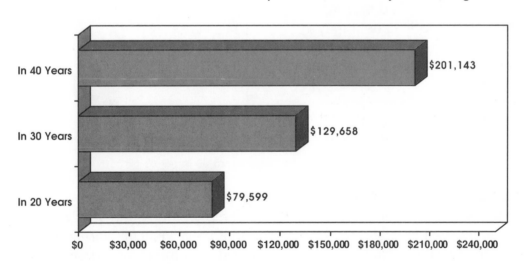

Inflation throws a real curve ball. Specifically, $79,599 will be needed in 20 years to equal $30,000 today. When the couple reaches age 75, they will need $129,658 in order to have the purchasing power of $30,000 today. At age 85, the couple will need $201,143 in order to have the purchasing power of $30,000 today. If you think this sounds absurd, consider the impact of inflation on a postage stamp. A 6¢ stamp in 1972 had the same buying power as a 29¢ stamp in 1993.

3

Adding the $79,599 and each subsequent inflation-adjusted value can be startling. The 20-year cumulative total of inflation-adjusted values equals $2,632,015. Even if the couple adjusted their deposits upward with inflation each year (5% in this example), they would still need to save $17,078 in the first year. This realization, or "future shock," is often experienced as people move into their retirement years.

The impact of time and interest on money is an amazing phenomenon. The rule of 72 is a shorthand method to help you estimate how long it will take to double your money. You can also apply this rule to determine how long it will take for inflation to reduce an asset in half. The formula is 72 divided by the interest rate, which equals the number of years needed to double your money. Consider an example where you can earn 10% per year. Applying the formula, 72 divided by 10 equals 7.2. Your money doubles in 7.2 years.

Get Started

The message is clear. You must take control of your financial future. What you don't know will hurt you. Who else can you count on to take care of the older person you will someday be? You may be thinking, why start today? The sooner you start, the more you will accumulate.

Consider the graph to the right. You save $2,000 per year and earn a consistent 10%. Startling as it may seem, you will have more money at age 65 saving from age 21 to 28 than from age 29 to 65.

The power of an early start is absolutely essential for your financial plan.

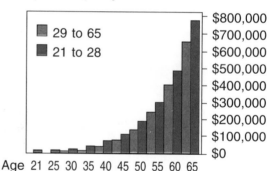

$2,000 per year at 10%

■ 29 to 65
■ 21 to 28

$800,000
$700,000
$600,000
$500,000
$400,000
$300,000
$200,000
$100,000
$0

Age 21 25 30 35 40 45 50 55 60 65

The Six Perspectives of Financial Planning

The six perspectives of financial planning can help you focus on your financial goals. This concept is based on the premise that your financial plan is only as strong as the weakest link. Consequently, considering the following six perspectives will help you ensure a rock solid financial plan.

1. If I live, is my plan based on sound principles?
2. If I become disabled or die, is my plan still solid?
3. Are my assets protected from lawsuits?
4. Does my plan minimize the effect of taxes?
5. What happens to my plan in an emergency?
6. Will my plan provide for a secure retirement?

Sound Principles
A sound principle is a financial strategy that will stand the test of time. Diversifying your portfolio is one example of a sound principle. Other sound principles are discussed throughout this book.

Disability and Death Protection
Inadequate income replacement protection can wipe out a financial portfolio with amazing speed. Your future goals should be achieved regardless of your ability to constantly go to work. Similarly, your death could leave your family in a terrible financial mess. A good plan guarantees that the people you love can always count on you -- even if you should become disabled or die.

Asset Protection
The United States has 7% of the world's population and 70% of the world's attorneys. Protecting your assets from lawsuits is more important than ever. Furthermore, this book will explain techniques that may help you achieve asset protection in the event of bankruptcy or property loss.

Minimizing Taxes
Taxes have a massive impact on your net spendable income. Understanding what taxes are today and what they are likely to be in the future is critical. You will learn six tax reducing strategies. Furthermore, this book will teach you how to grow funds tax-deferred and access them tax-free.

Emergency Access
Emergencies are inevitable. If you fail to plan for emergencies, you will continually dip into your intermediate and long-term assets. Keeping debt under control is essential. This book will help you establish the correct amount of emergency funds for your financial plan.

Retirement Planning
Financial independence is often associated with successful retirement accumulation. Retirement and other financial goals usually involve a long-term holding period or investment span. This book will help you to put distractions that change constantly, like current investment earnings, in perspective and teach you to focus on performance consistent with your investment span.

The six perspectives help you maintain your focus and "watch your flanks." This seems so simple, but why is it that so many people fail to plan their finances in a disciplined and organized manner?

Snapshots in Time

I'm 25 and I have plenty of time until I retire. The priority is to get settled in a career and buy a new car. Besides, I barely make enough to cover my expenses. I deserve to have fun while I'm young. I will retire when I am 50.

I'm 30 and saving for the future is important, but right now I need to focus on buying a home. I've finally finished paying off student loans and now I'm going to get serious about my credit card debt. I will retire when I am 55.

I'm 35 and the mortgage and child care payment consumes the bulk of our earnings. Furthermore, the costs of raising children seem to take every penny we earn. When the kids are older, it will be much easier to save. My goal is to retire when I reach 60.

I'm 45 and the cost of sending the children to college is setting us back several years. I will have to start saving for retirement after they finish school. If I save every penny, I should be able to retire modestly when I am 65.

I'm 55 and the children have all finished school. The mortgage is almost paid off. I really could use a new car. I need a review of my plan for retirement. For the first time in my life, I am starting to wonder if I will ever be able to retire.

I'm 60 and the money I have saved in the last few years is just starting to grow. Unfortunately, my savings would only last a year or two if I stop working today. I am very concerned about the risk of needing nursing home care someday.

I'm 65 and investing is a great idea, but Social Security doesn't go very far. I should have started years ago, but it's too late now. I hope I never need nursing home care because I can't afford to even think about it. There are few things in life I regret -- but failing to floss my teeth and saving for my retirement are two I'd never repeat.

Sound familiar? You can succeed if you get started today. Take the time to take the first step and learn what action is necessary to achieve financial success. *Perfect Money Planning* is written to help you establish where you are now and what you need to do to achieve your goals.

Thinking about the future is an appropriate way to begin a financial plan. Your perception of the future will directly affect the decisions you will make.

Taxes in the Future

Do you feel a future upper tax rate in excess of 50% is realistic? When considering future tax rates, it is useful to review past tax rates. You may be surprised to know that the historical average is 61%. While a historical review is interesting, current events and political administrations have a significantly greater impact on current tax rates. Today, there are three primary reasons for a likely increase in future tax rates. These are the national debt, Social Security and the increasing demand for nationalized health care.

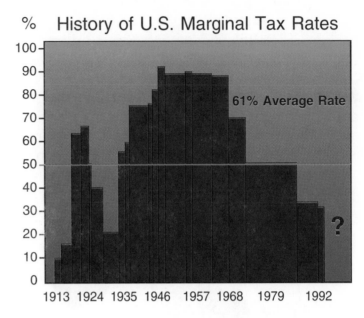

The National Debt

Economists agree that the national debt adversely affects the financial stability of the United States. Taxes appear to be the primary source of funds available to help pay this debt.

Social Security

Most people unknowingly plan on living on a nine-digit income at age 65. Unfortunately, the nine digits many people plan on are the nine digits on their Social Security card. Social Security may provide you some benefits, but will definitely leave a large gap that only you can close.

When Social Security was created, life expectancy was projected to be age 62. The selection of age 65 ensured a system that would be self-sustaining. The advent of life expectancies well beyond age 65 has raised many questions about the strength of the Social Security system. The average recipient of Social Security today receives every penny contributed plus interest in just three years. The average recipient is receiving benefits from Social Security for over 12 years. The sad reality is that the ultimate price may be paid by younger Americans who will not get back their fair share because it has already been spent.

The current 100% retirement benefit minimum age has already been postponed for many Americans.

Social Security

Year of birth	Retirement age
Before 1938	65
After 1937 but before 1955	66
1955 and later	67

Source: Internal Revenue Code Section 415(b); Social Security Act Section 216 (l).

Will Social Security be postponed again in the future? Will you have to wait until you are 71 to receive the 100% benefit in the future? Demographic studies provide additional insight to these questions. Demographic projections clearly indicate America is aging. The impact of the aging of America on Social Security is profound.

By the year 2000, there will be one person on Social Security for every three people working. By the year 2030, this ratio will be almost one to one.

Nationalized Health Care

Health care consumes a substantial share of the gross national product. A *Forbes* article recently predicted that national health-care costs will increase nearly sevenfold by the year 2010. Furthermore, the movement for nationalized health care is increasing in intensity each day. Many health care analysts predict that within the decade all Americans will have health care provided as a basic right. The funds to pay for this may come from income taxes. Nationalized health care alone could increase your current tax bite.

Tax Trends?

Taxes like the 15% "success" tax and 20% required withholding on pensions may become more common. The "success" tax is an excise tax that is imposed on excess distributions from a qualified retirement plan.

The 15% excise tax is triggered by aggregate distributions that exceed the greater of $112,500 adjusted for inflation or $150,000 (Internal Revenue Code Section 4980A(c)(1)). Today, most people taking distributions from a qualified plan avoid the "success tax." Nonetheless, many people are surprised to learn that they will receive less than they had expected from their qualified retirement plan. Qualified retirement plans are lucrative targets for future government revenue.

Another indicator supporting this trend is the 20% required withholding on rollovers from IRAs or qualified retirement plans. The 20% required withholding became effective January 1, 1993 and applies to distributions made to a participant from a qualified pension plan. Trustee-to-trustee transfers bypass the 20% tax. This withholding was designed to create funds to pay for unemployment compensation continuation legislation passed in 1992. An example will help you better understand this new tax.

Steve has a retirement plan at work with a $10,000 balance. Steve leaves his employer to start his own business. Steve decides to take possession of his $10,000 and roll this money within 60 days to an Individual Retirement Account (IRA) in order to avoid taxation. The trustee of Steve's retirement plan at work sends Steve a check for $8,000. The trustee is required by law to send 20%, or $2,000, to the IRS.

Unless he can get a refund within 60 days from the IRS, Steve will be responsible for income and 10% penalty taxes on the $2,000. Steve has one other option. He can use money from another source to bring his IRA account balance to $10,000 and avoid taxation. This tax may seem hard to believe, but the 20% required withholding is a strong indicator of a trend that may make qualified retirement plans less desirable.

Please pay the IRS this amount

In estate planning, you can currently pass $600,000 of assets estate tax free to your children. The rumblings out of Washington suggest a reduction in the size of a tax-sheltered estate and increased taxation of Social Security benefits. The point is clear--be prepared to pay more taxes.

Tax-deferred vehicles, as a potentially lucrative source for government revenue, may suffer considerably in the years to come. The Perfect Money Plan will consist of a mix of tax-deferred and tax-free funds. In high tax years, you would access your tax-free funds. In low tax years, you would access taxable funds.

One positive note is that laws in the future are usually not retroactive to the past. The significance of this point is that a good tax-shelter today will likely continue to serve you well into the future. This concept is commonly referred to as "grandfathering."

The Banking System in the Future

The Savings and Loan failures of the 1980s and 1990s have left society with a significant burden. As historians continue to study the ramifications of this debacle, the government may impose greater limitations on amounts guaranteed in banks. The Federal Deposit and Insurance Corporation may, in the future, disallow more than one claim, regardless of the fact that you had your money invested in more than one bank. Insurance for deposits above $100,000 may be available at a cost.

Life Expectancies Increase?

As technology continues to advance, it is reasonable to expect life expectancies to continue to increase. You probably think you will only live as long as your parents. More likely than not, you will live longer than your parents. In the future, major organ transplants will be routine occurrences. Will you have the funds necessary to take advantage of tomorrow's technology? Fortunately, financial vehicles are also improving at a rapid rate. Your life insurance death benefit could realistically be the source of funds to pay for an operation to save your life.

Unconventional Phases in Life

Increased life expectancies may translate into unconventional life patterns. For instance, it may become common for people in their fifties and beyond to return to college. A 60-year-old retiree may decide to return to work and start a new family. The traditional path of marriage, work and then retirement may no longer exist. Consequently, the traditional risk assumptions are correspondingly dynamic. No longer can you assume that you will be safe to take on more or less risk at a given age. Therefore, financial vehicles that allow you to change risk and reward components at little or no cost will be of greater value. The assumption that family protection needs terminate at a given age may also be less valid than in your parents' lifetime.

Self-Appraisal Questions

	Yes	No
1. Taxes will increase?	___	___
2. Living to age 90 or 95 will be normal?	___	___
3. A larger percentage of Americans will be poor in the year 2010 than are poor today?	___	___
4. Will people live dynamic life styles, such as retiring and starting a family?	___	___

5. Inflation will average _____% over the next 20 years.

6. I plan to retire at age _____.

A written financial plan is an important ingredient for financial success. A financial plan is a map for your money. Most people agree that maps are often essential to accomplishing a significant goal. Consider a mountain climber without a map. Why risk wasting time, getting lost and possibly never accomplishing your goal? The point is simple--attempting to achieve financial success without a financial plan reduces your probability of success.

Financial planning is cost effective. Proper financial planning saves you time and money.

Establishing an Emergency Fund

One of the first steps in creating a financial plan is to establish an emergency fund. Your emergency fund should range from three to 12 months' income. If you are conservative, create an emergency fund equal to at least six months' income.

The long-term benefit of an emergency fund is that your funds dedicated for retirement continue to grow untouched in the event of an emergency.

Establishing a Contingency Day

You should select one day each year for a contingency planning day. Contact your financial consultant to review and update your financial plan. Review your legal plans and ensure that your family knows where your important documents are located.

My Contingency Day is _____

Take the time to ask yourself each of the six perspective questions discussed in the Introduction. You owe it to the people you love to spend at least as much time planning for their security as you do planning for their vacation.

Now that you have established a contingency day, you need to know where you are now. You will then be able to set realistic goals for your future.

Financial Organization

Understanding your cash flow is essential. The following worksheet will help you determine where your money is going and how much you can start investing. You may wish to use this worksheet annually and watch your net worth increase.

Cash Flow Worksheet

Monthly income:

Your salary _____

Spouse's salary_____

Other pay _____

Dividends _____

Interest _____

Rental property_____

Social Security _____

Pension benefits_____

Annuities _____

Alimony _____

Other _____

Total monthly

income: $_____

Monthly expenses:

Mortgage or rent _____

Homeowners insurance _____

Life, health and
other insurance _____

Taxes _____

Installment purchase _____

Food _____

Home maintenance _____

Utilities and fuel _____

Clothing _____

Transportation _____

Entertainment _____

Travel/vacations _____

Clubs and organizations _____

Charity and gifts _____

Alimony _____

Miscellaneous _____

Total monthly

expenses: $_____

Income minus expenses

equals $_____

Net Worth Statement

Assets:

Savings accounts _____

Checking accounts _____

Certificates of deposit _____

U.S. Savings Bonds _____

Life insurance (cash value) _____

Annuities (cash value) _____

IRA account _____

Pension (vested interest) _____

Securities (market value) _____

Real estate (market value) _____

Business interest _____

Personal property _____

Other _____

Total assets: $_____

Liabilities

Mortgage (balance due) _____

Taxes _____

Installment loans _____

Charge account _____

Charitable pledges _____

Other _____

Total liabilities: $_____

Total assets: $_____

  minus

Total liabilities: $_____

Net worth: $_____

Based on a brief review of where you have been (net worth) and where you are going (cash flow), are you happy with your financial success? How much more would you like to save each month?

_____

_____

_____

_____

_____

Determining Your Priorities

Your specific goals will dictate your priorities. Occasionally, simultaneous goals result in confusion and indecision. The financial instrument hierarchy pyramid helps you decide what action to take first. In a given situation, certain financial products will be more important than others. For instance, if you do not own health insurance and are given the choice of buying health insurance or investment art, you would choose health insurance. Common sense dictates a need for health insurance is more important than buying art. The same logic can be applied between the various levels of the following diagram.

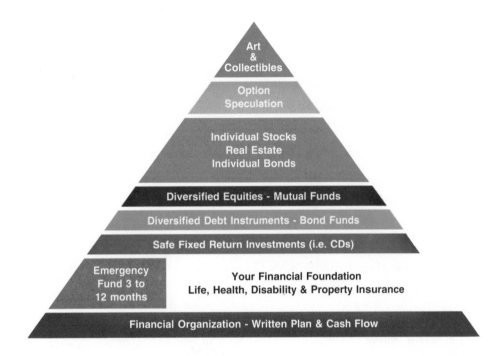

A well-designed financial plan will first identify where you are now and where you want to be in the future. After determining your cash flow, the foundation of your financial future must be established. Subsequent layers will then be built on a solid lower layer, ensuring a secure structure.

Imagine the person who buys 1,000 shares of ABC stock without first establishing an emergency fund. The decision to sell shares of ABC will now be dependent on when the car breaks or some other financial crisis arises.

The financial hierarchy philosophy is based on the fact that the risk of death, accident, sickness, or disability can cause a financial disaster at any moment. Therefore, the core elements of your financial foundation must be addressed prior to investing in stocks. The key point to remember about insurance is that you must buy it when you do not need it. When you need insurance because you have already suffered a loss, you cannot buy it.

Setting Goals

Place a check mark next to the goals that are important to you. Prioritize goals in order of their importance to you. You may wish to use a pencil for this exercise.

Important	Goal	Priority
☐	Establish an emergency fund.	_____
☐	Establish a Contingency Day on _____.	_____
☐	Protect my family financially.	_____
☐	Guaranteed income replacement if sick or hurt.	_____
☐	Have a comfortable retirement.	_____
☐	Save and invest systematically.	_____
☐	Complete a financial plan.	_____
☐	Protect my assets from the risk of a lawsuit.	_____
☐	Take advantage of tax-favored vehicles.	_____
☐	Protect my finances in the event of long-term nursing care.	_____
☐	Provide funds for my children's education.	_____
☐	Accumulate funds for _____.	_____
☐	Minimize my tax bite.	_____
☐	Avoid estate taxes.	_____
☐	Review my plan or specific program.	_____
☐	Establish health care for myself and/or family.	_____
☐	Obtain better property & casualty protection.	_____
☐	Start my own business.	_____
☐	Other _____.	_____

List your three most important goals:

1._____

_____

2._____

_____

3._____

_____

Impending Changes

You need to consider significant changes that may impact the financial planning process. For instance, a promotion may increase the amount you will be able to comfortably save. Check the following changes that may apply to you in the next two years.

Change	Projected Date
☐ Marriage	_____
☐ New home	_____
☐ Children	_____
☐ Sell property	_____
☐ Inheritance	_____
☐ Salary increase	_____
☐ Pay off loans	_____
☐ Go back to school	_____
☐ Bonus	_____
☐ Promotion	_____
☐ Change job	_____
☐ Lose job	_____
☐ Start business	_____
☐ Sell business	_____

Financial Professionals

Searching for names of financial professionals can be difficult. Take time now to list the financial professionals who work for you at present.

Title	Name	Phone Number
Accountant	_____	_____
Banker	_____	_____
Financial Consultant	_____	_____
Insurance Agent	_____	_____
Securities Broker	_____	_____
Attorney	_____	_____
Other	_____	_____

Personal Asset Inventory

An excellent way to document your possessions is to videotape them. Written lists are ideal, but involve a lot of work. Most people can satisfy their documentation needs with an annually-updated 30-minute videotape. Date your videotape for insurance purposes with the help of the U.S. Post Office. Send your video to yourself and open the package in the event of a claim only when you have your insurance adjuster present.

Your Legal Documents

You should certainly have a will. If you have children, you should also identify a guardian for them. Another important document is a living will. A living will provides guidance should you be on a life-support system and have no chance of recovery. Make time to meet with your attorney to satisfy your legal needs.

A living trust is a useful estate planning tool to avoid probate. A living trust is a written agreement that creates a trust that can own property and conduct business. Living trusts are *inter vivos*, or created during life. A knowledgeable financial consultant will help you identify your need for a living trust and other legal services. Be careful to choose an attorney who specializes in estate planning if you are considering constructing a living trust.

Debt for the individual is a financial trap that steals freedom. Avoiding debt is extremely difficult, due to the fact that advertisers bombard us with hundreds of promotions every day. Without a conscious plan, debt avoidance is almost impossible.

The following story serves as an illustration of the danger of buying now and paying later. Imagine a family in a burning theater. The father says to his family, "Stay here, I'll be back in a moment after I help our local car dealer out of the theater." In a moment, the father returns and again instructs his family to wait, for he is going to help the man who is about to install the family's new pool. The fire has just engulfed three of the four walls. The father comes back again to instruct his family to wait still longer, while he helps his travel agent reach safety.

While this story may seem unrealistic, most people actually save for the future in a similar manner. Most people spend money on things that are less important than their family's need for financial security. A key to avoiding debt is to pay yourself first by saving a percentage of every paycheck. Consider how often saving is delayed only to buy a pool or take a vacation.

Credit Cards

Credit cards make obtaining debt easy. The more credit cards you own, the greater the opportunity for overspending. Interest rates on credit cards usually range from 12% to 22%. Three simple guidelines will help you keep credit cards under control.

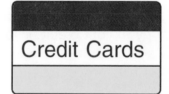

1. Have at most one or two major credit cards. Look for cards that are accepted worldwide and have minimal fees. Seek billing procedures that allow you to pay up to 30 days after the monthly statement without incurring interest charges, if no outstanding charges exist. Some cards are available without annual fees and a small fraction of your billing is paid back to you. Once you have determined the one or two cards you need, cancel your credit line with all other credit card companies. The immediate benefits range from saving on excessive charges to reducing your risk in the event of theft of your cards. One other immense benefit-- the fewer the cards you have, the less you will use them.

2. Never use a credit card to spend money you do not have. Credit cards are convenient tools to pay for purchases. Credit cards save you from the risk and worry of carrying large sums of cash. Buyer protection assurances are valuable and a useful credit card benefit. Learn to use your credit card only to purchase items that you can completely pay for in that same month. Always avoid rolling your credit card balance from one month to another.

3. Each month, check the accuracy of your statement against the receipts you have saved. This simple step will help remind you of the real money you are spending. The obvious second benefit is that you will verify your billing for accuracy.

Married couples should agree on the upper limit that each person can spend without consulting each other. This simple measure can go a long way in managing your debt and preserving your marriage.

Qualifying for Credit

The underwriting process for credit involves a close analysis of your payment history in the last three to five years. If you have defaulted on an agreement or experienced bankruptcy, you can count on that information remaining on your credit report for ten years.

There are several ways to verify credit. One way is to call Bankcard Holders at 1-703-481-1110 or write them at 560 Herndon Parkway, Suite 120, Herndon, VA 22070. Should you disagree with the report, you can request an investigation. Bankcard Holders can help you initiate a correction. Regardless of the outcome of the investigation, you are entitled to submit a 100-word statement defending yourself. Your statement will be provided with all future reports regarding your credit history. If you have been turned down for credit in the last 30 days, the report will be provided free. Otherwise, plan on spending approximately $35 for a copy of your credit history.

Car Loans

Another common use of credit is to purchase an automobile. Five rules will help you avoid making big mistakes.

1. Instead of getting a loan to buy a new car, could you keep what you have or buy a used car instead? Do not think of a car as an investment. A car is likely to depreciate 10% the moment you drive it off the lot. Even a car kept in good shape may lose half its original value after five years.

2. Call three different lending institutions to determine the annual percentage rate they charge. Pay special attention to how the rate is applied.

3. When possible, choose a loan with a shorter term. Each year of interest payments increases the cost of your car considerably.

4. Ask for a detailed listing of all charges or costs associated with the loan. Avoid credit life and additional loan protection whenever possible. You can usually cover your need for protection more efficiently. Many of the ways to do so are covered in Chapter 5.

5. Be sure to understand if prepayment penalties apply. You may be surprised to find additional charges or accounting methods which would raise your effective interest rate.

Home Equity Loans

Interest on home equity loans is tax deductible up to $100,000 total debt. Home equity loans are risky for two reasons. The first is that you may have to sell your home to pay your debt. The second is that your home may decline in value, leaving you with negative equity. Unfortunately, homeowners sometimes end up paying money to sell their home due to negative equity. A home equity loan is generally not an advisable strategy to fund college education costs or other wealth accumulation goals. In some states, creditor protection laws may protect a home from creditors. In these states, home equity loans as a practical matter do not exist.

Complete the next two exercises and quiz to obtain a true picture of your debt.

Total Your Debt

Creditor	Payment Each Month	Total Interest Paid Last Month	Interest Rate Being Charged
1.			
2.			
3.			
4.			
5.			
6.			
7.			
8.			

Total $_____ $_____

Personal Debt Ratio (Debt to Earnings)

Example:

$$\frac{\$396}{\text{Total debt each month} \atop \text{(excluding mortgage)}} \div \frac{\$3,300}{\text{After-tax income} \atop \text{each month}} = \frac{12\%}{\text{Debt Ratio}}$$

$$\frac{}{\text{Total debt each month} \atop \text{(excluding mortgage)}} \div \frac{}{\text{After-tax income} \atop \text{each month}} = \frac{}{\text{Debt Ratio}}$$

Debt Ratio Analysis

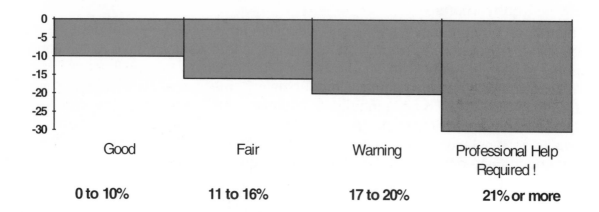

Good	Fair	Warning	Professional Help Required !
0 to 10%	11 to 16%	17 to 20%	21% or more

If you have a debt ratio other than good, you should immediately begin to reduce your expenditures and eliminate your debt.

Quiz - Are you over your head in debt?

Answer the following questions as they best apply to your specific situation.

	Always	Sometimes	Never
1. Are bills paid using money previously allocated for another purpose?			
2. Are repayment schedules extended from 30 to 60 or 90 days?			
3. Are loans taken to repay old loans?			
4. Are credit limits at or near the maximum?			
5. Do you incur credit card interest charges?			
6. Are emergency funds below 3 months' income?			
7. Are bills paid late?			
8. Do you bounce checks?			

If you scored eight "never" answers, then you have your debt under control. If you scored a mix between "never" and "sometimes," you can benefit tremendously from the information in this chapter. If you scored a mix of "sometimes" and "always," professional assistance is advisable. If you scored eight "always" answers, seek credit counseling help immediately. Remember, credit is not designed to buy things you don't need with money you don't have in order to impress people you don't know.

Advice for Those Drowning in Debt

You should inform your creditors of problems immediately. Your next course of action is to contact the nonprofit Consumer Credit Counseling Service. Counselors offer free budget planning and assistance in administering debt repayment. Call the National Foundation for Consumer Credit at 1-800-388-2227, or write them at 8611 Second Avenue, Suite 100, Silver Spring, MD 20910. Beware of firms advertising "quick fixes" or charging fees of $500 or more.

A debt consolidation loan may help you dig your way out. If you decide to consolidate your debt, consider a home equity loan because the interest payments are tax deductible. Car loans pose a special problem because most financing agreements allow your car to be repossessed. The creditor will then resell the car and you are still responsible for paying the difference of what you owe minus the selling price.

Filing for Bankruptcy

Always get a second opinion before you file for bankruptcy. Unfortunately, some professionals prey upon people under this type of financial pressure. Bankruptcy is rarely in the best interest of the person considering this option. Be extremely careful when considering bankruptcy.

There are two forms of personal bankruptcy: Chapter 13 and Chapter 7. Chapter 13 filing is usually preferable because it allows retention of personal property. To qualify under Chapter 13, you must owe less than $100,000 unsecured or $350,000 secured and have a regular income. The court will protect you from collection efforts and all finance charges will stop. The court will dictate that all or a portion of the debt be repaid over a period of three to five years.

The second and more severe form of bankruptcy is Chapter 7. Filing this form of bankruptcy asks the court to release you from your obligation to repay your debt. The court will most likely seize every asset within reach. Filing under Chapter 7 is a virtual guarantee that you will be denied credit for the next ten years.

Creditor-Proof Assets

Understanding basic creditor-proof planning is important, even if you have excellent debt management. With the number of attorneys increasing each year in the United States, the chance of being involved in a lawsuit is greater than ever. A recent study determined that we have seven percent of the world's population and seventy percent of the world's attorneys. Are your assets safe?

A personal liability lawsuit judgment or settlement could wipe out your financial plan. What would you do if you permanently disabled another person in a car accident? Would your retirement plans crumble? You can acquire protection in excess of your auto or homeowner limits with a personal catastrophe liability policy. A personal catastrophe liability policy is commonly called an umbrella policy.

An umbrella policy is designed to help you guard against catastrophic liability losses caused by the following incidents:
1. Lawsuits and liability claims exceeding your auto and homeowners coverage.
2. Damage to the property of others.
3. Bodily injury to others.
4. Slander, libel and other types of personal injury.

An umbrella policy is an excellent tool to reduce the risk of your assets being seized. Many insurance companies offer $1,000,000 of umbrella coverage for under $250 per year.

There are several other ways to creditor-proof assets. State laws have a significant impact and, consequently, you need to consult a qualified attorney. For instance, life insurance is 100% exempt from the claims of creditors in Texas under Senate Bill 1261. The state-to-state variations are significant and you should be aware of the laws in your own state. The following may offer protection from creditors in your state.
1. Life insurance cash value (even mutual fund based life insurance).
2. Employer-sponsored retirement plans.
3. Assets placed within a creditor-proof trust.
4. Your home.

Federal Taxes

The federal tax system can be classified into two categories: Federal Income and Transfer. The federal income tax is the dominant burden for most people.

The federal income tax is a tax on the income you earn and on investment income. The rates for 1993 are 15%, 28% and 31%. Tax brackets are adjusted annually for inflation.

Example: A married couple has taxable income of $36,900. How much income tax do they owe (assuming no exemptions or deductions)? The answer is $5,535 (see Married and Surviving Spouses table). If they have $50,000 in taxable income, they would owe $5,535 plus an additional 28% on amounts over $36,900. The total tax due equals $9,203, or $5,535 plus $3,668. The additional $3,668 is derived from $50,000 minus $36,900 equals $13,100. The $13,100 is multiplied by 28% and equals $3,668.

Married And Surviving Spouses

Taxable Income Over	But Not Over	The Tax Is	Of The Amount Over
$0	$36,900	15%	$0
$36,900	$89,150	$5,535 + 28%	$36,900
$89,150	N/A	$20,165 + 31%	$89,150

Unmarried Individuals

Taxable Income Over	But Not Over	The Tax Is	Of The Amount Over
$0	$22,100	15%	$0
$22,100	$53,500	$3,315 + 28%	$22,100
$53,500	N/A	$12,107 + 31%	$53,500

Heads of Households

Taxable Income Over	But Not Over	The Tax Is	Of The Amount Over
$0	$29,600	15%	$0
$29,600	$76,400	$4,440 + 28%	$29,600
$76,400	N/A	$17,544 + 31%	$76,400

Married Filing Separate

Taxable Income Over	But Not Over	The Tax Is	Of The Amount Over
$0	$18,450	15%	$0
$18,450	$44,575	$2,767.50 + 28%	$18,450
$44,575	N/A	$10,082.50 + 31%	$44,575

The personal and dependency exemption for 1993 is $2,350 for individuals.

The standard deduction follows:

Married and Surviving Spouses	$6,200
Unmarried Individuals	$3,700
Heads of Households	$5,450
Married Filing Separate	$3,100

According to the IRS, the average American works until May 8th just to pay federal, state and local taxes. Is your projected Federal Income Tax four or five months' income (including Social Security tax)?

Projecting Your Taxes

Total Annual Income (include your salary, tips, dividends, interest income, taxable Social Security and all other taxable income).

_____

Exemptions (exemptions are allowed for the taxpayer, spouse and dependents).

minus _____

Adjustments (deductible SEPP contributions and 401(k) (self-employed), IRA contributions and alimony payments).

minus _____

Adjusted Gross Income or AGI (subtract exemptions and adjustments from total annual income).

equals_____

Itemized Deductions. Actual deductions may be determined by itemizing on Schedule A. Consult your tax advisor to determine your itemized deductions and limitations that apply. The following is a brief list of expenses that are generally deductible.
- Mortgage interest
- Charitable contributions
- State and local taxes paid

equals_____

Total Taxable Income (subtract itemized deductions from adjusted gross income).

equals_____

Total Tax (refer to the tables on page 23 to calculate your tax).

equals_____

The previous calculation will be an accurate projection for most taxpayers. If tax credits apply to your situation, simply reduce your total taxes due dollar for dollar. Highly-compensated people should verify that no additional tax liability applies. The most common additional tax is the Alternative Minimum Tax.

Federal Income Tax Strategies

Tax Justice

You should seek the professional services of a Chartered Financial Consultant, Certified Financial Planner or tax advisor if you believe tax avoidance planning will be of benefit to you. The penalty for improper application of tax avoidance strategies is severe and, consequently, you need to be absolutely sure your plan is in compliance with the Internal Revenue Code. Understanding basic tax strategy terminology will help you evaluate the importance of tax avoidance as part of your financial plan. There are six categories of tax strategies: prepay, transfer, incentive, deferral, deduction and conversion.

Prepay
The prepayment strategy is a conscious decision to incur tax today at a lower rate than you anticipate having in the future. Prepayment strategies also include techniques to fund for future tax liabilities. Two common prepayment planning techniques are investment insurance overfunding and estate liquidity funding.

Transfer
This technique is sometimes called the deflection technique. The strategy is to transfer taxes to someone with a lower tax bracket. For example, gifting to children used to be popular. The Federal Transfer Tax and changes to the Federal Income Tax (gifting to minors) have eliminated a lot of the appeal of tax transfer.

Incentive
An incentive is a tax law that provides for special tax treatment. Investment tax credits are examples of tax incentives.

Deferral
Deferral is a tax postponement technique. You will have to pay taxes in the future. By deferring taxes, your funds grow faster. One potential danger of deferral is that a 10% early withdrawal penalty often applies (prior to age 59½). Another potential danger is that your future tax rate may be higher. An analysis of the positive effect of more funds compounding sooner, offset by the tax on the income stream, is necessary to make an informed decision on whether or not to defer taxes.

Deduction
A tax deduction reduces current taxable income. A common example is an Individual Retirement Account. Taxes are due on the entire balance in the future. Retirement-related tax deductions expose you to the same pitfalls discussed in the tax deferral section.

Conversion
Conversion involves converting ordinary income into something different. Municipal bonds, capital gains and home sales may present opportunities for income conversion. For instance, when you sell your home, you may recognize the gain or convert the gain into a new home within two years of selling your original home.

Federal Transfer Tax

The Federal Transfer Tax is a tax on transferred property. Estate and gift taxes are types of transfer taxes. The Federal Estate Tax is a tax on property transferred at death. The Federal Gift Tax is a tax on property gifted during life. The tax brackets are identical for Federal Estate and Federal Gift taxes. The Generation Skipping Tax is a flat 50% tax. This tax is imposed on transfers to grandchildren in excess of the $1,000,000 exemption. The Generation Skipping Tax is in addition to Federal Estate and Federal Gift taxes.

The following table will help you **calculate** your estate and gift taxes.

Column 1 Taxable Gift or Estate From	To	Tax on Column 1	Tax on Excess
$0	$10,000	$0	18%
$10,000	$20,000	$1,800	20%
$20,000	$40,000	$3,800	22%
$40,000	$60,000	$8,200	24%
$60,000	$80,000	$13,000	26%
$80,000	$100,000	$18,200	28%
$100,000	$150,000	$23,800	30%
$150,000	$250,000	$38,800	32%
$250,000	$500,000	$70,800	34%
$500,000	$750,000	$155,800	37%
$750,000	$1,000,000	$248,300	39%
$1,000,000	$1,250,000	$345,800	41%
$1,250,000	$1,500,000	$448,300	43%
$1,500,000	$2,000,000	$555,800	45%
$2,000,000	$2,500,000	$780,800	49%
$2,500,000	$10,000,000	$1,025,800	50%
$10,000,000	$18,340.000	$4,775,800	55%
$18,340,000	....	$9,362,800	50%

A unified credit of $192,800 applies to estate taxes. This means that estates under $600,000 in value are tax sheltered. The table on the previous page is designed to help you project gift or estate taxes. Consult a tax advisor for a more accurate assessment.

An Estate Planning Example

Palma Rowleys owns a $2,500,000 business and another $500,000 in personal assets. Palma also owns a $100,000 life insurance policy. Palma's liquid assets for estate tax payment purposes (including the life insurance death benefit) total $250,000. Palma is a 50-year-old widow. If Palma were to die, what would happen without an estate plan? Would Palma's daughter, Jane, take over the business? Would Palma's 20 employees still be able to work at the factory?

The life insurance is income tax free, but included in the estate for Federal Estate Taxes. Assume for the sake of simplicity that the taxable estate in this situation is $3,100,000. Applying the tax table on page 26, the estate tax is $1,325,800. The $1,325,800 is then reduced by the $192,800 unified credit. The end result is an estate tax payable of $1,133,000.

Had Palma and her deceased husband created, prior to his death, a unified credit trust to receive estate assets equivalent to the unified credit at his death, the assets in that trust would then pass free of estate tax to Jane at Palma's later death. Use of this basic estate planning technique enables a married couple to pass the equivalent of $1,200,000 estate tax free to their heirs. In our example, let's assume that the Rowleys had created a unified credit trust prior to the husband's death. The end result is that the estate tax payable at Palma's death is reduced to $833,000, for a savings of $300,000 in estate taxes.

The IRS demands payment from the estate's executor within nine months. However, Palma's estate has only $250,000 in liquid assets to pay the $833,000 estate tax bill. As a result, Palma's executor may have to sell the business in order to generate the remaining $583,000. The executor may find that a forced liquidation generates far less than the fair market value of the business. Jane may only inherit one-third or less of her anticipated estate.

If the Rowleys had planned for the estate's liquidity needs, this devastation could have been avoided. A second-to-die insurance policy could have generated the needed $583,000 tax free, assuming that the policy was owned by a third party, such as Jane or an irrevocable life insurance trust. Otherwise, the total estate value and corresponding tax bite increase.

If a second-to-die life insurance policy had been purchased while Palma's husband was still alive, the total outlay would have been $51,992 or less. This assumes at the time of purchase that he was in good health and age 49, while Palma was age 47. The $51,992 represents the cumulative premiums to the abbreviation point for a top company's second-to-die plan. The $51,992 would provide permanent protection, regardless of when death occurred. Since most people make payments in increments, such as annually ($5,357 in this example), the total outlay would be less if death occurred prior to the abbreviation point. In this situation, since Palma's husband died after three years, the total outlay would have been $16,071. The diagram below, however, assumes that the full $51,992 payment had been made prior to his death.

No Estate Plan	With Estate Plan		
Estate $3.1 M	$2,500,000 Taxable Estate - $250,000 Liquid Assets	$833,000 Estate Tax - $250,000	
	$2,250,000 - $51,992 →Insurance→	$583,000 - $583,000	
Tax $1.13 M	$2,198,008 + $600,000 Trust Assets	$0	
	$2,798,008 **Total to Jane**		
Jane $1.97 M	Jane $2.8 M	Jane receives $831,008 more!	

Sound too good to be true? Well, it is easy to explain. The joint life expectancy for Palma and her husband is over 38 years. The insurance company will earn far more than $583,000 on that $51,992 deposit. For instance, $51,992 at 8.5% for 38 years equals $1,154,161.

When planning for estate taxes, there are four methods of payment to consider. The first method is to accumulate enough cash in your estate to pay estate settlement costs outright. The second method is to borrow the cash to pay estate settlement costs. This only defers the problem, since the money will have to be repaid with interest. The third way is to liquidate sufficient assets to pay estate settlement costs. A forced liquidation may bring only a small fraction of the true value, if there is not a ready market. The fourth method is to pay your estate settlement costs with "pennies on the dollar." For every dollar your estate needs, you give an insurance company ½ to 5 cents a year (depending on your age) for a limited period of time.

For single people, a single-life policy can create similar leverage. One final note, many financial consultants agree that it is the smaller estates that can least afford not to plan for the transfer of assets.

Life Insurance and Its Tax Advantages

Most people misunderstand life insurance. Everyone has an opinion, but few people really understand how life insurance works. The development of life insurance in the 18th century can help you understand life insurance today.

Prior to 1760, only limited duration life insurance was available. A mathematician named James Dodson was denied this "term" coverage because he was 46 years old.

Dodson was motivated to create insurance that would protect a person for his or her whole life. Dodson created a way for people to obtain permanent or whole life insurance. The essence of this revolutionary idea can be summed up this way: deposit a small amount of money regularly and when you die, your family will receive a large amount. Should you not die prematurely, you will get back more money than you deposited.

To begin, all life insurance plans can be broken into three components: mortality, administration and investments. Mortality cost is defined by an actuarial table that projects the number of people with similar characteristics who die each year. Administration cost involves every expense in managing and servicing the plan. The investment account is an accumulation fund. The premium paid less mortality and administrative expense is credited to the investment fund.

The range of available life insurance plans is vast. An in-depth understanding of the life insurance components will help you select superior life insurance plans. Refer to Chapter 10 for assistance on choosing a financial consultant and an insurance company.

Mortality

A significant cost component in a life insurance program is the mortality cost. Mortality cost is derived from tables developed by actuaries and approved for use by state insurance authorities. Actuaries are mathematicians who carefully study and project future occurrences based on quantitative data. Hence, they project as accurately as possible the number of people who will die in a given year at a given age. Consider the following table found in frequent use today.

1980 Commissioner Standard Ordinary Table

Age	Male	Female		Age	Male	Female
0	4.19	2.89		50	6.71	4.96
1	1.07	.87		51	7.30	5.31
2	.99	.81		52	7.96	5.70
3	.98	.79		53	8.71	6.15
4	.95	.77		54	9.56	6.61
5	.90	.76		55	10.47	7.09
6	.85	.73		56	11.46	7.57
7	.80	.72		57	12.49	8.03
8	.76	.70		58	13.59	8.47
9	.74	.69		59	14.77	8.94
10	.73	.68		60	16.08	9.47
11	.77	.69		61	17.54	10.13
12	.85	.72		62	19.19	10.96
13	.99	.75		63	21.06	12.02
14	1.15	.80		64	23.14	13.25
15	1.33	.85		65	25.42	14.59
16	1.51	.90		66	27.85	16.00
17	1.67	.95		67	30.44	17.43
18	1.78	.98		68	33.19	18.84
19	1.86	1.02		69	36.17	20.36
20	1.90	1.05		70	39.51	22.11
21	1.91	1.07		71	43.30	24.23
22	1.89	1.09		72	47.65	26.87
23	1.86	1.11		73	62.64	30.11
24	1.82	1.14		74	58.19	33.93
25	1.77	1.16		75	64.19	38.24
26	1.73	1.19		76	70.53	42.97
27	1.71	1.22		77	77.12	48.04
28	1.70	1.26		78	83.90	53.45
29	1.71	1.30		79	91.05	59.35
30	1.73	1.35		80	98.84	65.99
31	1.78	1.40		81	107.48	73.60
32	1.83	1.45		82	117.25	82.40
33	1.91	1.50		83	128.26	92.53
34	2.00	1.58		84	140.25	103.81
35	2.11	1.65		85	152.95	116.10
36	2.44	1.76		86	169.06	129.29
37	2.40	1.89		87	179.55	143.32
38	2.54	2.04		88	193.27	158.18
39	2.79	2.22		89	207.29	173.94
40	3.05	2.42		90	221.77	190.75
41	3.29	2.64		91	236.98	208.87
42	3.56	2.87		92	253.45	228.81
43	3.87	3.09		93	272.11	251.51
44	4.19	3.32		94	295.90	279.31
45	4.55	3.56		95	329.96	317.32
46	4.92	3.80		96	384.55	375.74
47	5.32	4.05		97	480.20	474.97
48	5.74	4.33		98	657.98	655.85
49	6.21	4.63		99	1000.00	1000.00

On the basis of the above table, you could accurately project that out of the general population of 1,000 30-year-old men, 1.73 will die each year. Ignoring the other expenses, the effects of underwriting and investments, $100,000 of insurance would cost $173 per 30-year-old person per year (1.73 per thousand x 100 units of protection).

Since mortality charges comprise a significant part of life insurance costs, make sure that you are classified correctly. The difference between a smoker and a non-smoker is significant. Most companies will reclassify you as a non-smoker if you have discontinued smoking for one year. Other medical conditions are also subject to review. If you are unsure about your mortality charges or underwriting classification, contact a financial consultant today.

If you currently own life insurance, compare your policy's mortality table with the 1980 CSO. You will gain a better understanding if you compute a few age and cost per thousand calculations.

Administration

The main components in the administration or expense category are policy administration, policy design, adherence to state regulation, marketing, and legal services. Some of the costs are fixed, while other costs are variable. Examples of fixed costs are policy design and state regulation filing. Examples of variable costs are commissions and policy administration. Fixed costs are lower per contract when a large number of contracts are sold.

Investment

Since the 18th century, relatively little change occurred in the way life insurance plans were structured. The investment component has changed drastically in the last few years. The best way to understand how the investment component works within a life insurance contract is to consider each type of plan separately.

Term Insurance

Term insurance offers no savings component. The cost of term insurance is the sum of the mortality and administrative expenses minus the interest an insurance company earns for investing the premiums. Consequently, this simplicity makes it very desirable to many people. The major drawback of term insurance is that coverage exists only for a specific period of time. Renewal options appear attractive, but usually become prohibitively expensive as an individual gets older. You may find yourself one day out on a limb that will eventually break.

Whole Life Insurance

Whole life insurance, also called permanent insurance, combines the term insurance with a cash value or savings element that grows on a tax-deferred basis. The premium charged for this protection is based on mortality, expenses and investment assumptions that produce a guaranteed cash value equal to the initial insurance amount at the insured's age 100.

Universal Life Insurance

Universal life insurance was born when the high interest rates of the early 1980s (18% CDs) far surpassed the intermediate and long-term bond holdings at that time. Universal insurance has an investment component that will only reflect short- to intermediate-term interest rates. Since all insurance except term is generally considered a long-term investment, the underlying investment portfolio is often inconsistent with most consumers' time horizon.

Variable Life Insurance
Variable life insurance is often called investment insurance. Investment insurance is a combination of term insurance and mutual funds. The contract owner can direct the investment selection. When properly configured, investment insurance offers whole life or permanent lifetime protection.

The variable life insurance vehicle is very powerful. As you go through various life cycle changes, such as retirement and returning to work, variable life insurance allows you to fine tune your investment mix. The product for today and for tomorrow for many educated consumers is variable insurance. Due to the investment flexibility, double digit returns are possible.

This diagram illustrates the results of $1 invested in common stocks, bonds, and at the rate of inflation. Clearly the winner consistent with a long-term time frame is common stocks.

Investment Performance
1926 - 1991

Annual Returns
Common Stocks 10.3%
Bonds 4.6%
Inflation 3.2%

$593
$18
$8
$1

1926 1936 1946 1956 1966 1976 1986 1991

Source: <u>Stocks, Bonds, Bills and Inflation 1991 Yearbook</u>™, Ibbotson Associates, Chicago.

Accelerated Benefits

The accelerated benefit has been called the biggest change in the life insurance industry since Dodson invented permanent insurance. In effect, you become your own beneficiary. The death benefit is paid to you in the event you need a major organ transplant, are terminally ill or require permanent nursing home care.

Be careful to closely evaluate a contract's accelerated death benefit. Look for contracts that do not charge a fee for this benefit. A superior contract will have no upper limit for terminal illness and pay out the present value of the death benefit. For instance, if you are terminally ill and expected to live another six months, you would receive over 90% of the death benefit. Superior contracts that provide funds for nursing home care usually provide approximately 70% of the death benefit immediately.

This concept was developed by an insurance company executive who was inspired by the plight of a man in an AIDS hospice. The patient wished to live his last days in dignity. The executive searched for a way to make the man's life insurance proceeds available to help him with his treatment. The executive thought "why not pay this man his death benefit now and simply offset the cost by discounting the insurance benefit for the few months interest the insurance company will lose." This simple idea has revolutionized the life insurance industry.

The mechanics of this benefit are easy to understand. Consider the real-life story of a Dallas man, age 31. This man's work-related injuries necessitated an immediate heart transplant. Unfortunately, his health insurance company would only pay a fraction of the cost. He did not have the savings to pay. Prepared to die in days, this man called his insurance agent and was ecstatic to learn that his $150,000 life insurance policy could be immediately paid to him, less an interest charge. The man collected his death benefit, paid for his new heart, and used the remaining funds to pay off his mortgage. Often major organ transplant recipients can buy life insurance after recovery at higher, but usually reasonable rates.

Term life insurance without accelerated death benefits should be replaced if alternate coverage with this benefit can be obtained. If you own a whole life or permanent plan, you should consult your financial consultant. Generally, replacement of existing permanent protection is not to your benefit. You may want to consider an additional policy to satisfy your need for the accelerated death benefit.

A Look at the Mechanics

The mortality curve or probability of death is the same regardless of the plan of insurance. Understanding the internal mechanics of term, whole life, universal and investment life insurance will help you conclude which type or combination is best for you.

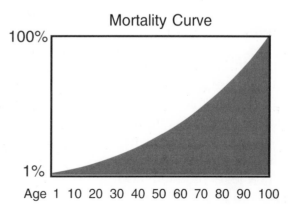

Mortality Curve

Term Life

In a term policy, the amount at risk is identical to the death benefit. Term insurance premiums equal the amount at risk multiplied by an age specific mortality factor. Administration expenses are added and the final premium is determined. For each year older a person becomes, the premium is increased to the new age-specific mortality factor. The actuarial probability of death for insurance purposes is usually at age 100.

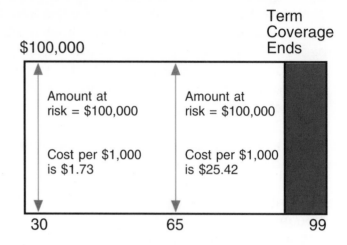

Cost of insurance at age 30 is 100 units x $1.73 or $173
Cost of insurance at age 65 is 100 units x $25.42 or $2,542

Due to this ever-increasing cost, most plans terminate before death. Unfortunately, the need does not terminate, and many families are left without proper protection.

According to a Penn State University study, only 1.8% of all term plans ever deliver a benefit payment to a beneficiary. The 1.8% statistic should cause concern because 98.2% of the contracts eventually terminate and many families are left without protection. Term insurance is essentially temporary insurance.

1.8% Payoff Ratio!

Whole Life

A whole life plan is designed to build cash value which reduces the amount of insurance at risk. Each year the chance of death is greater, but the amount at risk decreases due to the increase in cash value.

The insurance company is collecting a premium above the mortality and administration cost and guarantees a 4% return on that money. The result is to provide the insured with a product that has a level premium and cash accumulation. Mutual

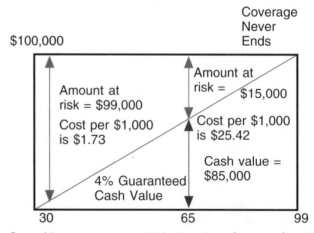

Cost of insurance at age 30 is 99 units x $1.73 or $171.27
Cost of insurance at age 65 is 15 units x $25.42 or $381.30

insurance companies are owned by their policyholders. Dividends are a combination of actual mortality, expense and investment results more favorable than those assumed in the policy. Stock companies may also pay dividends. Many mutual companies have paid dividends every year since inception.

Universal Life
The internal mechanics are similar to whole life, except the investment portfolio is a short-term interest-sensitive account. Unlike whole life insurance, the guaranteed return alone in a universal life policy is usually insufficient to sustain the policy for life.

Variable or Investment Life
The mechanics of investment life are similar to whole life and universal life. Investment life applies the strategy of buying term insurance and investing the rest under one umbrella. The combination results in the only diverse self-directed tax shelter to grow tax deferred and be accessible tax free.

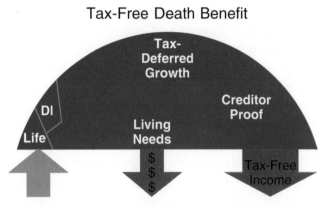

Tax-Free Death Benefit

The tax advantages of investment life insurance are many. The mechanics of term insurance and whole life insurance will help you understand variable or investment life insurance.

This diagram illustrates the cost per 1,000 multiplied by the amount at risk of insurance. The remaining funds are deposited into a mutual fund account. As the investment increases from 7% to 9%, the number of insurance units decrease. Eventually a "corridor crunch" occurs (see diagram).

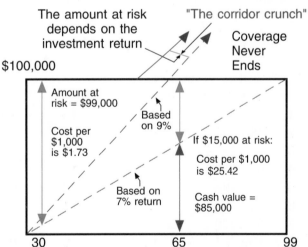

Cost of insurance at age 30 is 99 units x $1.73 = $171.27
Cost of insurance at age 65 is 15 units x $25.42 = $381.30

The "corridor crunch" allows the life insurance contract to maintain its definition as life insurance. This is important because life insurance is a tax-favored vehicle.

The end result is a vehicle that grows tax deferred and provides tax-free access to funds (withdraw contributions and borrow the gain).

Consider the following example of two investments at the same rate of return. Both investments are fixed-rate returns earning a consistent 9.5%. In both alternatives, $4,000 is invested for seven years (a total of $28,000). The investor in this example is a 35-year-old male. Surprisingly, he would have more money over time in the insurance contract (see the table below). The U.S. Government has just paid for this person's entire insurance program.

How is this possible? Refer to the table below and calculate the taxes in year 16 for the certificate of deposit. The $66,757 at 9.5% earns $6,341.92. Assuming 28% taxes, this person would pay $1,775.74 in taxes. The total accumulation in year 17 is $71,323. The investment insurance fund also earns 9.5%, but is not subject to taxes. The total insurance account value in year 17 is $80,092. The spread in favor of investment insurance becomes greater and greater as more funds are added to the two alternatives. If taxes go up in the future, this tax shelter becomes more and more valuable.

The investment insurance accumulation is less than the CD accumulation in the initial years. That is due to the fact that the insurance cost exceeds the taxes in the first few years. In this example, it takes the insurance contract 11 years to catch up. If more money is invested sooner, the insurance contract will exceed the CD accumulation much faster.

Another point to remember: the insurance contract offers benefits beyond the investment accumulation, such as the death benefit.

The Accumulation Power of Investment Insurance
(Male, Select, Preferred, $100,000 death benefit, Age 35, 9.5% consistent return)

Year	CD Fund	Insurance Fund	Year	CD Fund	Insurance Fund
1	$4,274	$2,888	16	$66,757	$73,303
2	$8,840	$7,044	17	$71,323	$80,092
3	$13,718	$11,584	18	$76,201	$87,475
4	$18,930	$16,544	19	$81,413	$95,501
5	$24,498	$21,963	20	$86,982	$104,224
6	$30,447	$28,117	21	$92,932	$113,794
7	$36,803	$34,823	22	$99,288	$124,287
8	$39,321	$37,904	23	$106,079	$135,782
9	$42,010	$41,244	24	$113,335	$148,357
10	$44,884	$44,864	25	$121,087	$162,092
11	$47,954	$48,607	26	$129,370	$176,819
12	$51,234	$52,673	27	$138,219	$192,858
13	$54,738	$57,084	28	$147,673	$210,315
14	$58,483	$61,870	29	$157,774	$229,304
15	$62,483	$67,061	30	$168,565	$249,934

Taxes on the CD exceed the insurance cost on the investment insurance plan. The investment insurance plan would net an additional $81,369 at age 65. Uncle Sam has paid for the entire cost of the insurance.

Overfunding an investment insurance contract may generate greater income than a qualified retirement plan. This is dependent on future tax rates and your specific situation.

The following example will help you understand the power of investment insurance as a non-qualified retirement plan. Assume individual taxes are 34% (federal 31% and state taxes equal to 3%) in the future and no special treatment or penalty applies to the qualified plan distributions. Contributions to the plan are based on 15% of compensation. The owner, Susan, has two employees.

Name	Compensation	Contribution
Susan	$200,000	$30,000
Bob	$100,000	$15,000
Mike	$26,666	$4,000

If Mike is in the 28% tax bracket, the $4,000 is equivalent to $5,555.55 contributed to a personal after-tax investment program. The $4,000 qualified contribution would likely accumulate faster than an overfunded investment insurance contract. If Mike retires to a significantly higher tax bracket, the result may be different. The significant point for Mike to understand is that he will likely need to save more than $4,000 per year to accomplish his retirement goal. In this scenario, an overfunded investment insurance plan may be the ideal complement.

If Susan is interested in providing benefits only for herself, the situation can be very different. In her 34% tax bracket, a $30,000 tax-deductible contribution is equal to a $45,455 taxable contribution. In this situation, a $30,000 tax-deductible contribution is approximately equal to a $30,000 after-tax contribution for Susan. That is, plan administration and mandatory employee contributions would otherwise consume the $15,455 in pre-tax savings, since Susan would have to contribute the same 15% to a qualified plan for her employees Bob and Mike. While the employee contribution and plan administration expense are tax deductible, the combination of mandatory employee contributions and plan administration would consume Susan's $15,455 tax savings.

A business owner in this situation can benefit from permanent life insurance protection, accelerated death benefits, waiver of premium disability benefits and potential creditor protection, while simultaneously increasing retirement income. The following analysis assumes Susan is a smoker and the additional cost for the insurance is reflected.

The Accumulation Power of Investment Insurance
(Female, Select, Standard, $2,000,000 death benefit, Age 35, 9.5% consistent return)

Year	Deposit	Retirement Income	Insurance Fund	Qualified Plan
1	$30,000	N/A	$8,193	$32,850
2	$30,000	N/A	$36,210	$68,821
3	$30,000	N/A	$66,770	$108,209
4	$30,000	N/A	$99,826	$151,339
5	$30,000	N/A	$135,620	$198,566
6	$30,000	N/A	$178,927	$250,279
7	$30,000	N/A	$225,492	$306,906
8	$30,000	N/A	$275,651	$368,912
9	$30,000	N/A	$329,727	$436,809
10	$30,000	N/A	$388,118	$511,156
11	$30,000	N/A	$447,622	$592,565
12	$30,000	N/A	$512,347	$681,709
13	$30,000	N/A	$582,792	$779,321
14	$30,000	N/A	$659,485	$886,207
15	$30,000	N/A	$742,983	$1,003,247
16	$30,000	N/A	$848,862	$1,131,405
17	$30,000	N/A	$965,265	$1,271,738
18	$30,000	N/A	$1,093,282	$1,425,404
19	$30,000	N/A	$1,234,098	$1,593,667
20	$30,000	N/A	$1,389,144	$1,777,915
21	$30,000	N/A	$1,561,083	$1,979,667
22	$30,000	N/A	$1,751,083	$2,200,586
23	$30,000	N/A	$1,961,050	$2,442,491
24	$30,000	N/A	$2,192,908	$2,707,378
25	$30,000	N/A	$2,448,489	$2,997,429
26	$30,000	N/A	$2,724,827	$3,315,035
27	$30,000	N/A	$3,028,917	$3,662,813
28	$30,000	N/A	$3,363,676	$4,043,630
29	$30,000	N/A	$3,732,483	$4,460,625
30	$30,000	N/A	**$4,138,770**	**$4,917,234**

It's no surprise that the qualified plan accumulates more wealth.

The bottom line is not what you accumulate, but what you can spend. The $4,138,770 investment insurance fund can provide a greater retirement standard of living than the $4,917,234 qualified plan. A specific analysis is always required because no one solution is always superior. If taxes are lower than 34%, the qualified plan can come out on top. Since future tax rates are likely to be in excess of 34%, individuals as well as business owners should consider diversifying retirement accumulation plans between qualified and non-qualified sources of income. The overfunding of an investment insurance contract is commonly referred to as a non-qualified plan or private pension plan.

What you accumulate is nice, what you keep is even better.

Age	Net After-Tax Retirement Income	Insurance Fund	Qualified Plan
65	$360,884	$4,158,048	$4,837,578
66	$360,884	$4,178,786	$4,750,354
67	$360,884	$4,200,508	$4,654,843
68	$360,884	$4,222,408	$4,550,259
69	$360,884	$4,244,183	$4,435,740
70	$360,884	$4,265,223	$4,310,341
71	$360,884	$4,284,609	$4,173,030
72	$360,884	$4,300,650	$4,022,673
73	$360,884	$4,311,971	$3,858,033
74	$360,884	$4,317,075	$3,677,753
75	$360,884	$4,315,382	$3,480,345
76	$360,884	$4,305,945	$3,264,184
77	$360,884	$4,286,864	$3,027,487
78	$360,884	$4,256,814	$2,768,305
79	$360,884	$4,215,413	$2,484,500
80	$360,884	$4,162,179	$2,173,733
81	$360,884	$4,095,446	$1,833,444
82	$360,884	$4,012,899	$1,460,827
83	$360,884	$3,911,535	$1,052,811
84	$360,884	$3,786,108	$606,035
85	$360,884	$3,634,722	$116,814
86	$360,884	$3,456,853	($418,883)

A 34% tax bracket is used for all calculations. The distribution methodology for the insurance fund is to withdraw the amount contributed, then borrow the gain from the insurance fund over a 22-year time frame. The investment insurance contract is not surrendered.

The investment insurance performs better in this circumstance. Amazingly, the cost of the insurance benefits is actually less than the cost of the taxes on the qualified plan distribution. Ask yourself, what is the chance that Susan will retire to a tax rate in excess of 34%? What if Susan hires two more employees? What happens if Susan lives beyond 86? Positive answers to any of these questions widen the spread in favor of the investment insurance contract.

While the qualified pension plan has long since been depleted, the investment insurance plan offers tremendous benefits at age 95 and beyond.

Funds Available At 95 if:	Insurance Fund	Qualified Plan
You Died	$8,079,893	Spent
You Were Terminally Ill	$7,271,904	Spent
You Went To A Nursing Home	$5,655,904	Spent
You Needed A Major Organ Transplant	$7,271,904	Spent

On December 14, 1992, the IRS proposed making accelerated death benefits tax-free distributions. The accelerated benefit values above reflect tax-free treatment. There is one additional point to consider. Susan was assumed to be a smoker in this example. If Susan had stopped smoking, the values shown would have increased due to the lower mortality cost associated with non-smokers.

In conclusion, an investment insurance plan can provide great benefits, whether you live, die, become disabled, experience bankruptcy or need the accelerated death benefits. Chapter 9 describes the private pension plan's benefits in detail.

How Much Insurance Do You Need?

Before you begin to calculate your insurance needs, consider the following story. You are driving home and a drunk driver in a Rolls Royce runs a red light. You are hit and killed in this accident. How much should your family seek in retribution from this wealthy drunk driver? Certainly you would want the present value of all your future wages for your family. You probably are imagining a figure of a million dollars or more.

Now imagine the story is changed and you have fallen asleep at the wheel. How much would you leave behind to care for your family? Would the dollar value on your life be the same as in the first example? Do you agree that it should at least be close?

Many people are unclear as to whether or not they have adequate life insurance. A good way to determine your insurance need is to determine the amount that would continue your income for your family. You should also consider your family's cash needs in the event of your death. A knowledgeable financial consultant can help you consider circumstances unique to your situation and, thereby, establish a much more accurate level of protection. Social Security survivor benefits, company benefits and other assets available to meet your insurance need should be considered.

Add up your cash and income needs with the following exercise.

Calculate Your Life Insurance Need

	In the event of your death, your spouse needs?	In the event of your spouse's death, you need?
Immediate Money Fund (Medical and hospital expenses, burial expenses, attorney's fees, etc.)		
Debt Liquidation		
Emergency Fund (Unexpected needs, etc.)		
Mortgage Payment Fund		
Child/Home Care Fund		
Educational Fund		
Capital Needed To Replace Income (Divide income by rate of return; e.g., $20,000 / 8% = $250,000)*		
Subtotal		
Total Current Life Insurance		
Total Other Assets (you would like to have go toward meeting your insurance needs)		
New Capital Required (Subtract total current life insurance and other assets from subtotal)		

*To determine a more accurate value, the present value of the capital needed to replace income can be entered.

Inflation and Your Life Insurance

If your need for insurance has not changed, you probably still need to buy more. The impact of inflation is significant and cannot be ignored. The following chart illustrates the effect of inflation on $250,000 from 1982 to 1990. The Consumer Price Index is the basis for the applied inflation.

Year	Original Amount Owned	Current Amount Needed To Maintain Purchasing Power	Percentage Increase Required
1982	$250,000	$365,000	46 %
1983	$250,000	$352,500	41 %
1984	$250,000	$340,000	36 %
1985	$250,000	$327,500	31 %
1986	$250,000	$315,000	26 %
1987	$250,000	$312,500	25 %
1988	$250,000	$297,500	19 %
1989	$250,000	$285,000	14 %
1990	$250,000	$272,500	9 %

Disability Insurance Protection

Normally your income exceeds your expenses and you have a cushion of savings. The moment a disability occurs, you begin to see income decline and expenses increase. How long would your savings last if you were sick or hurt and could not go to work. Protect your greatest asset -- your ability to earn a living.

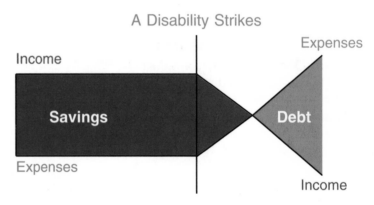

The Question

If you had a goose that laid golden eggs, would you insure the goose or the eggs? If you are like most people, you would insure the goose because the goose can replace the eggs.

Your ability to earn a living can be thought of in a similar manner. Your car and house are usually insured, yet your income is often left uninsured.

The probability of being disabled for three months or longer before reaching age 65 is relatively high.

For example, a 35-year-old stands a better than 50% chance of being disabled for 90 days or longer prior to reaching age 65.

If you are sick or hurt, how will you continue to pay your mortgage and other living expenses? How long would your savings last? Assuming you recover, would you be able to replace your savings and retire as you had planned?

Disability insurance can be complex, and the services of a qualified financial consultant should be sought.

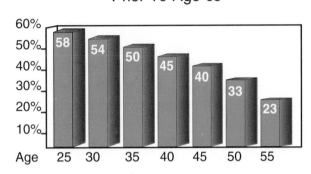

Your Probability of Disability Prior To Age 65

Source: 1985 Commissioners Individual Disability A Table

The Social Security Administration provides disability benefits. Due to the strict definition of disability, however, never count on receiving Social Security disability. The Social Security Administration denies over 65% of all claims.

More homes are foreclosed on due to a disability than any other reason (49%). Income replacement planning is essential.

Foreclosed
Owner Disabled
House For Sale
49%

Disability income plans can be one of the most cost-effective insurance programs you can own. Consider the following analogy. Almost everyone insures their car, which may cost $2,000 a year. If you totaled your car, you might get back $25,000 (the value of your vehicle). That same $2,000 in a disability income plan might pay over $1,000,000 tax-free in income benefits.

The following checklist will help you make sure your income replacement plan is in order.

Feature	Discussed Yes/No	Feature	Discussed Yes/No
Definition of disability		Automatic benefit increase	
Duration of benefits		Association discounts	
Waiting period for benefits		Hospital income benefit	
Inflation adjustments to benefits		Recovery benefit	
Residual benefits		Rehabilitation benefit	

Feature	Discussed Yes/No	Feature	Discussed Yes/No
Future income options		Premium refund option	
Social Security guarantee		Reduced waiting options	
Cosmetic surgery benefits		Death benefits	

You should consider the difference between group and individual disability protection. Group disability insurance is usually more restrictive than individual coverage. Applying the checklist from the previous page to your group coverage may uncover several large gaps in coverage. Furthermore, unlike group plans, individual disability plans replace your income on a tax-free basis.

Dollar for dollar, a disability income plan can be a tremendous value and an important part of your financial plan.

Property and Casualty Insurance

Take the time to meet with a property and casualty insurance agent. Special care must be taken to make sure coverage and deductibles are correct. An agent who meticulously services your account can save you time and money. A basic understanding of auto and homeowners insurance can help you be aware of potential gaps in your coverage.

Auto insurance consists of four major types of coverage. The first is liability insurance, which includes bodily injury and property damage liability. Bodily injury protection covers injury to passengers in your car, to people in other cars, and to pedestrians. Most people need $100,000 per person and $300,000 per accident for bodily injury coverage. Property damage liability covers damage to property owned by someone else. Most people need to choose a minimum of $100,000 in property damage liability.

The second coverage is collision protection. Collision covers damage to your car when you have hit or been hit by another vehicle or object. The third coverage is comprehensive protection. Losses covered by comprehensive insurance are theft, falling objects, glass breakage and fire, to name a few. The fourth major coverage is uninsured motorist coverage. Uninsured motorist coverage protects you in the event you are hit by an uninsured or hit-and-run driver.

To verify that you are paying the correct amount for auto insurance, you should understand how premiums are calculated. Insurance companies calculate your premium based on five general categories.

The first, rating territory, is the area in which you live. The higher the population density, the higher the probability for accidents, and thus the premium you pay is likely higher. The second is your driver classification. Drivers are classified according to their sex, age and marital status. Single men for instance tend to have more accidents than married men at the same age. The third category is your driving record. A person with three tickets should expect to pay more for auto insurance than a similar person with no tickets. The fourth category is the type of car you own. A luxury car or sports car would cost more to insure than an economy car. The fifth, use of car, is important because a car you use for pleasure and business is at risk a greater amount of time than a car you use for pleasure alone.

The five rating categories can be offset by the five discount categories. Inquire with your insurance agent about driver training, good driver, multi-car, anti-theft, and senior citizen discounts. Ask your insurance agent to review each page in your insurance contract with you.

A few tips on homeowners insurance can save you time and money. The first is to make sure you purchase replacement value coverage on your home and contents. Most policies require that you keep your coverage within 80% of the actual value of your property in order to qualify for replacement at 100% of the current value. A second tip is to make sure unique or very valuable property is scheduled on a personal articles floater. A third point, videotape your property because you will only be reimbursed for property you can prove you lost.

A final item to check is combined account discounts. You can often obtain significant discounts by insuring your home and car with one insurance company.

Health Insurance

Most plans provided by your employer are superior to individual plans you can buy yourself. Your benefits coordinator is the first person to consult if you have questions about your medical benefits. If you must buy an individual health insurance policy, take the time to choose your insurance company carefully. The best plan is not always the plan with the lowest annual premium. The best plan is the one you can really count on to pay for your medical care when you are ill.

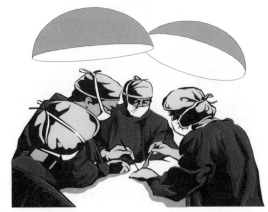

The Consolidated Omnibus Budget Reconciliation Act of 1985 (COBRA) requires that employees and certain beneficiaries be allowed to continue their current health insurance, at group rates, for up to 36 months following a qualified event. The act only applies to employers with 20 or more employees. Qualifying events for employees or the employee's spouse and children are:
1. The termination of an employee except for gross misconduct.
2. The death of the covered employee.
3. The divorce or legal separation of the covered employee and the spouse.
4. A child ceasing to be an eligible dependent under the plan.
5. The reduction in an employee's hours so that the employee or dependent is ineligible for coverage.

Employees wishing to take advantage of COBRA continuation must elect continuation within 60 days after a qualifying event. For employees who have employment terminated or qualify under a reduction in hours, an 18-month coverage continuation period exists. Other qualifying events trigger a 36-month coverage continuation period.

Solid medical plans are appropriately priced from inception. Appropriately-priced plans retain integrity as a risk group. Select your health insurance company as if it is the choice you anticipate making for life. If your health declines, you will find the extra dollars spent for a quality company to be a great value.

The concept of adverse selection is important to understand when selecting health insurance. Adverse selection is a process where a group of insureds becomes a higher risk group each year the plan continues. When insurance is priced too low, the insurance company has to drastically increase premiums to pay expenses. This increase results in healthy people leaving the group. The insurance premium continues to increase. The people who are not healthy cannot switch to a lower premium and, consequently, that risk group must pay a higher premium each year. Eventually, the premium is beyond what anyone can afford and coverage for all practical purposes terminates.

Long Term Care
The financial drain of nursing home care can be devastating. The American Association of Retired People or AARP is an excellent source of current information on long term care. You can call AARP at 1-800-523-5800 and request information.

Medicare
Medicare may pay many of your medical expenses when you reach age 65. The Medicare program has two parts. Part A is Hospital Insurance. Part B is Supplementary Medical Insurance. Part A coverage helps pay

for the cost of hospitalization, skilled nursing facility care, home health services and certain related inpatient care. Part B coverage helps pay for doctors' fees and outpatient services.

You qualify for Part A coverage on the basis of past work. Part B coverage is available at an additional premium. Substantial gaps in coverage exist and, consequently, many people seek Medicare insurance supplements. Contact your local Social Security Administration office for more information on Medicare and Medicare supplements.

Insurance You May Not Need

Most people need life, disability, health, auto, homeowners and umbrella protection (see Chapter 3 for information on umbrella protection). A financial plan can be wiped out in a flash if inadequate insurance is not established. Nonetheless, you may own insurance you do not need. Risk retention or self-insuring is sometimes the better solution.

When you buy insurance, you have decided to transfer your risk of loss. You have chosen to pay a predictable premium and eliminate the chance of severe hardship. Where many people go astray is when they purchase insurance for events that will not result in severe hardship.

Credit Card Insurance

Credit card companies often offer debt repayment programs in the event you die or become disabled. The cost per thousand for this type of coverage is often more than twice the going rate of a similar life or disability protection policy. Many cards offer to pay the minimum payment in the event you are terminated from your job. While this may seem appealing, a good financial plan will have a solid portfolio of life insurance, disability protection and emergency funds. When these core components of your financial plan are established, credit card insurance becomes an unneeded expense.

Flight and Accidental Death Insurance

Why would you need more life insurance if your death was caused by a plane crash instead of cancer? The amount of life insurance you provide for your family should not depend on how you die. Some people think accidental death insurance is a good deal because it is only a few dollars. The reason you can purchase $1,000,000 of flight coverage for $16 is simply because your chance of dying on your plane trip is a million to one. Gambling with life insurance is foolish.

Option to Purchase Additional Insurance

This coverage is often referred to by its abbreviation OPAI. OPAI guarantees you the right to purchase additional insurance at the same insurance classification (not age) you are eligible to receive today. OPAI is ideally suited for people with a family history of medical problems. The advent of AIDS has made OPAI coverage more valuable. You should discuss OPAI with your financial consultant to help you determine the value of this coverage to you.

Consumer Purchase Insurance

Extended warranty protection on appliances or other consumer goods is usually a risk that is best self-insured. Consider the probability that one in ten purchases will need servicing or repair. An extended warranty for ten items may cost as much as $250 per year. You are likely to spend more on warranties than you are on repairs.

Dread-Disease Insurance

Policies for cancer or specific illness usually provide very limited benefits with not so limited qualification requirements. A typical policy might provide an $80 a day benefit with an increase to $300 per day after 90 days in the hospital. Hospital stays for cancer average only 13 days (National Association of Insurance Commissioners) and will no doubt exceed the per day benefit provided. The higher benefit of $300 per day is rarely received because the majority of cancer care beyond the 13-day average is provided on an outpatient basis.

Student Accident Insurance

You can provide your child with very limited protection in the event of an accident at school. Student accident insurance is restrictive and often redundant. A ceiling of $25,000 is typical and will not go very far if a catastrophic injury occurs. Another severe limitation is the 12-month payment provision found in most policies.

The key to protecting your children is to have a solid health insurance plan. Student accident policies usually provide secondary coverage and, consequently, when all is said and done, you have paid for no benefit at all.

Understanding Risk, Holding Periods and the Erosion Effect

There are three factors you must understand prior to making an investment selection. These factors are risk tolerance, holding period and the erosion effect.

The first factor is risk tolerance. The risk level you are comfortable taking is a definite constraint on investment selection. Imagine you have $20,000 to invest each year and your goal is to accumulate $1,000,000. The following investments are available to you:

Risk	Net Return (31% Taxes)	Gross Return	Years To Goal
None	0%	0%	50
Low	5%	7.25%	25
Moderate	8%	11.59%	20
High	10%	14.49%	18
Very High	12%	17.39%	17

Ask yourself, are you willing to take a little risk to reach your goal 25 years sooner? How about a moderate risk to save five more years? If yes, then would you take a higher risk to save two more years? The question continues until you have found your risk/reward equilibrium.

The second factor is your holding period. To illustrate, one-year and 15-year holding periods of the Dow Jones Industrial Average were analyzed. The Dow Jones Industrial Average is a useful index for gaining a feel of past market trends. The publisher of *The Wall Street Journal* prepares the Dow Jones Industrial Average by monitoring a pool of 30 stocks which reflect total market value and broad public ownership. The average includes high-quality industrial stocks, which are likely to reflect overall market performance. Monitoring the Dow Jones Industrial Average can help you assess where the market is today relative to the past.

Dow Jones 1939 to 1991

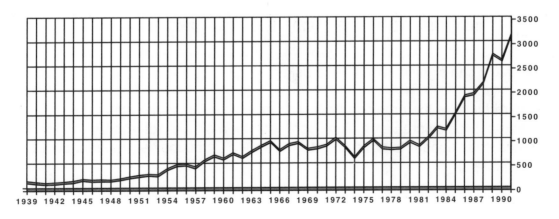

Consider the instability of one-year holding periods. The DJIA is a good representation of the volatility of the stock market over short periods of time.

**One-Year DJIA Holding Periods
(1940-1991)**

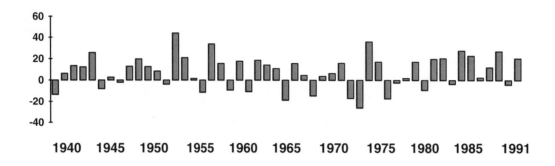

The volatility of the stock market is a primary reason why stocks are unsuitable as a low risk investment over a short-term holding period.

However, time can definitely reduce risk. Consider the DJIA over a 15-year period. Throughout the entire 41-year period, if you invested in the DJIA with a 15-year holding period, you would have never lost 1%.

**Fifteen-Year DJIA Holding Periods
(1950-1991)**

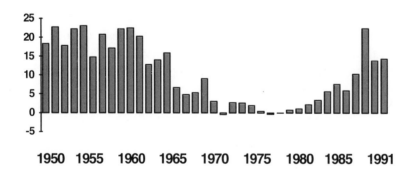

Time really can significantly reduce risk.

The third factor is the erosion effect. The erosion effect is the impact of inflation and taxes. Erosion creates a significant reduction on real returns. A CD, for instance, may appear to have an attractive yield, but consider the impact of the erosion effect.

Certificate of Deposit

Deposit	$10,000
If earns 7%	$700
Total	$10,700

Your real return is:

Gross return	7.00%	$10,700
Minus taxes (28% x 7%)	1.96%	$196
		$10,504
Minus inflation (20-year average)	6.00%	
Total year-end value	-.96%	$9,874

Inflation reduces the yield and, in this example, the combination with income taxes results in a net loss.

A Closer Look At Certificates of Deposit

Year	CD Rate	Tax Rate	Inflation	After Taxes and Inflation
1975	6.89%	64%	7.0%	-4.52%
1978	8.61%	64%	9.0%	-5.90%
1981	15.77%	63.2%	8.9%	-3.10%
1984	10.68%	49%	4.0%	1.45%
1987	7.01%	38.5%	4.4%	-.12%
1990	8.17%	31%	6.1%	-.46%

 This example applies taxes for an individual earning $120,000 per year. To obtain a better understanding of how tax-deferred or tax-free investments can increase your return, refer to formula below.

A tax-deferred investment would increase my return by:

$$\frac{\text{Interest Rate}}{(1-\text{Tax Bracket})} = \text{Tax-Deferred Equivalent} \quad \text{or} \quad \frac{8\%}{(1-30\%)} = 11.43\%$$

Complete your equation:

$$\frac{\_\_\_\%}{(1-\_\_\_\%)} = \_\_\_\_\_\%$$

The correct investment is consistent with your risk tolerance, holding period and attitudes regarding the erosion effect. Take time now to complete the following exercise.

Investment Selector

Investment Questions	Personal Objectives	Investment Category
What is the return you realistically require after taxes?	☐ 6% or less every year ☐ 6% to 8% every year ☐ 8% to 11% every year ☐ 11% to 15% every year ☐ 15% or more every year	Very High Safety Moderate Safety Some Risk Substantial Risk Extremely High Risk
How would you assess your risk tolerance on a scale of 1 to 9, with 1 being very conservative and 9 being very risky?	☐ 1-3 ☐ 4-5 ☐ 6-9	Safety Is Important Some Risk Substantial To Extreme Risk
If you had just won $10,000 in the lottery, which would you choose?	☐ Stocks ☐ Mutual Funds ☐ Certificate of Deposit	Substantial To Extreme Risk Some Risk Safety Is Important
What do you want your investment to do for you?	☐ Want no current income ☐ Want interest to grow ☐ Want to spend interest ☐ Want to spend principal	Growth Objective Income Objective
How do you feel about tax-favored investments?	☐ No interest ☐ Marginal interest ☐ Very important	Taxable Return Taxable Or Tax-Favored Tax-Favored
Why are you investing?	☐ Retirement ☐ For 10 years plus ☐ Sending child to college ☐ Purchase in 5 years ☐ Purchase in 3 years ☐ Purchase 3 years or less	Long To Very Long Long Intermediate To Long Intermediate Intermediate To Short Short Term
Do you have savings dedicated as emergency funds?	☐ 20% of income or less ☐ 40% of income or less ☐ 60% of income or more	Short Term Intermediate Long
Have you thoroughly reviewed your basic family protection plans and purchased adequate insurance?	☐ No ☐ Yes	Do not invest. Your basic insurance needs are the foundation on which a solid financial plan is built. Match the above responses to the investment selector grid on pages 55-56.

Investment Alternatives

Now that you have determined your risk tolerance and holding period, a basic understanding of the more common investment alternatives is essential.

Common Stock
A common stock is a share of ownership in a company. Stocks are sometimes referred to as equities. As depicted in the graph on page 60, stocks have outperformed bonds significantly over time. Stocks have historically had positive returns over 20-year holding periods. However, from a short range perspective, equities can be volatile and result in loss if holding periods are short.

Preferred Stock
A preferred stock pays a dividend that generally does not go up if the company's earnings rise. Preferred stockholders are entitled to collect their dividends before common stockholders. If dividends are cut, the common stockholders lose their dividend first. Preferred stockholders often have the right to collect skipped dividend payments.

Mutual Funds
Mutual funds are organized portfolios of many individual stocks or bonds. Mutual funds help you minimize the risk of owning individual stocks and bonds. The mutual fund investor does not randomly throw darts attempting to make the right investment decision. As a mutual fund investor, you can select a fund that matches your investment objectives.

Mutual funds are often classified as load or no-load funds. If you are unsure about which fund you should buy, a loaded fund will compensate a financial consultant for his or her time in helping you evaluate the fund that is right for you. The performance of a mutual fund is more important than the issue of load or no-load.

Mutual fund advantages are:
1. Professional management.
2. Diversification.
3. Exchange privilege.
4. Easy to understand and monitor reporting.

Bonds
Bonds are evidence of debt, either secured or unsecured by bondholders. Series EE and HH bonds are backed by the U.S. government and are very safe. The interest on both EE and HH bonds is exempt from state and local taxes. Interest on EE bonds is paid upon redemption. Interest on HH bonds is paid every six months and is included in ordinary income. For qualified investors, Series EE bonds may be redeemed tax free if the funds are used to pay for a child's college expenses. In order to qualify, married couples must have adjusted gross incomes of $60,000 a year or under; single people must have incomes of

Bonds allow cities and companies to raise money.

$40,000 or under. A proportionate scale applies to people in excess of the limit.

Owning a corporate bond makes you a creditor of a corporation. Corporate bonds can help you acquire a steady income stream. The degree of risk varies with the corporation issuing the bonds. Standard & Poors and Moody's rate the safety of bond issues. A convertible bond is a corporate bond that allows you to convert the bond into common stock. For most investors, a corporate bond mutual fund is recommended, because it allows you to obtain professional management and diversification.

A number of variables can affect the value of bonds. Bond price fluctuations are affected by market interest rates, maturity date, the debtor's financial stability, coupon rate, current yield and yield-to-maturity to name a few. Market interest rates are a primary variable in bond value changes. The market interest rate has a seesaw effect on bond values.

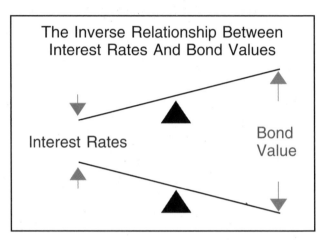

The Inverse Relationship Between Interest Rates And Bond Values

Interest Rates

Bond Value

Municipal Bonds
Municipal bonds are debt obligations of government institutions. Municipal bonds are free from federal income tax and, depending on the state in which you live, state income tax free. Municipal bonds can be very safe or very risky, depending on the municipality. An insured municipal bond is backed by an insurance company.

Government Securities
Government securities are bonds and securities issued or backed by the U.S. Government. The mix of bond, T-bills, notes and other money funds usually net a higher return than money market accounts.

Real Estate
Real estate is often a preferred long-term investment. Owning property involves more costs than most other investments. Nonetheless, real estate can be an excellent investment and inflation hedge.

Real Estate For Sale !

Venture Capital
Venture capital allows you to get in on the ground floor of business expansion. Venture capital is very risky and should be avoided by all but the most experienced investors.

Stock Options
Stock options provide you with the option to buy or sell shares of stocks. The vast majority of investors lose money in the options market. Unless you are a very experienced investor and willing to lose your entire investment, stay away from the option market.

Commodities
Commodities are binding legal agreements for the seller of these contracts to make delivery and the buyer of these contracts to take delivery of a commodity. The level of leverage and corresponding risk in commodities trading, such as pork bellies or soybeans, far exceeds the average investor's risk tolerance.

Gold, Precious Stones and Collectibles
Gold, precious stones and collectibles are investments for the knowledgeable investor. Tangible assets help to offset the impact of inflation, but are also less liquid than most other investments. A gold mutual fund allows you to reap the benefits without having to worry about storage and theft. The expertise of professional mutual fund managers in the tangible asset market is a definite plus.

Apply the investment alternative information to the fixed interest investments and mutual funds investment selector grid.

INVESTMENT SELECTOR GRID	High Safety	Moderate Safety	Low Safety	Long-Term	Intermediate-Term	Short Term	Tax-Favored	Taxable	Income	Growth 10% or Better
Fixed Interest Investments:										
CD	X					X		X	X	
Government Securities	X					X		X	X	
Fixed Annuity	X			X			X	X	X	
Corporate Bonds		X		X				X		
Municipal Bonds		X			X		X		X	
Zero Coupon Bonds		X		X				X		

INVESTMENT SELECTOR GRID	High Safety	Moderate Safety	Low Safety	Long-Term	Intermediate-Term	Short Term	Tax-Favored	Taxable	Income	Growth 10% or Better
Mutual Funds:										
Utility Fund		X		X	X			X		X
Stock Index Fund		X	X	X	X			X		X
Conservative Stock Fund		X	X	X	X			X		X
General Quality Bond Fund	X	X		X	X			X	X	
GNMA Fund		X		X	X			X	X	
High Yield Bond Fund			X	X				X	X	X
Global Stock Fund			X	X				X		X
Option Growth Fund			X	X	X			X		X

General guidance is useful, but specific offerings are different. Before making any investment, always read the prospectus and evaluate your risk tolerance, holding period and the erosion effect.

Now that you have determined where you should be, use the following investment checklist to specify the current value of each account. Next to the account value, enter the changes you would like to make to your plan.

Investment Checklist

Investment	Value of Account	Percent Increase	Percent Decrease	No Change
Checking Accounts				
Savings Accounts				
Certificates of Deposit				
Money Market Accounts				
Treasury Bills and Notes				
Life Insurance Cash Values				
Guaranteed Annuities				
Home Equity				
Bond Mutual Funds				
Stock Mutual Funds				
Variable Annuities				
Individual Bonds				

Investment	Value of Account	Percent Increase	Percent Decrease	No Change
Individual Stocks				
Real Estate				
Precious Metals				
Venture Capital				
Stock Options				
Commodities				
Collectibles				
Other				
Other				

Now that you have determined the correct asset allocation for you, contact your financial consultant to implement the changes you feel are necessary.

Dollar Cost Averaging

Dollar cost averaging (DCA) is a method of systematically saving and capturing the general trend of the stock market. DCA is a simple investment technique that reduces risk. DCA helps you benefit from the historical fact that a diversified portfolio of stocks has had positive returns over time. DCA requires that you deposit a predetermined amount of money at regular intervals, regardless of market conditions. The net effect is that you buy more shares when the market is low and fewer shares when the market is high. Buying more shares when the market is low is a basic principle of investment success.

DCA is an automatic technique that often outperforms many of the best market timers. DCA also affords you a greater degree of peace of mind, because the guess work of market timing is eliminated. Consider the following examples for an investor who decides to invest $500 a month under various market conditions. While these examples illustrate short-term results, DCA is most effective when applied as a longer-term investment strategy.

A Bear or Declining Market

Date	Regular Investment	Share price	Shares Acquired
Jan. 1	$500	$30	16.67
Feb. 1	$500	$25	20.00
March 1	$500	$20	25.00
April 1	$500	$15	33.33
May 1	$500	$10	50.00
June 1	$500	$5	100.00
Total	$3,000		245.00

On June 1, the investor's stock holding would be worth $1,225 ($5 per share x 245 shares). If sold, the investor's loss would be $1,775 ($3,000 initial investment - $1,225 current worth). However, if the entire $3,000 had been invested on January 1 at $30 per share, only 100 ($3,000/$30 per share) shares would have been purchased and the loss would have been $2,500 ($3,000 - ($5 per share x 100 shares)).

This example illustrates the fact that dollar cost averaging minimizes loss in a declining market.

A Bull or Rising Market

Date	Regular Investment	Share Price	Shares Acquired
Jan. 1	$500	$15	33.33
Feb. 1	$500	$20	25.00
March 1	$500	$25	20.00
April 1	$500	$30	16.67
Total	$2,000		95.00

In this example, on April 1 the DCA investment is worth $2,850 (95 shares x $30 per share), for a gain of $850 if the investment is sold. If the entire $2,000 had been invested on January 1, 133.33 shares would have been purchased. This investment would be worth $4,000 (133.33 shares x $30 per share), for a gain of $2,000 if sold. In a bull market, DCA captures a lesser gain.

In Fluctuating Markets

Date	Regular Investment	Share Price	Shares Acquired
Jan. 1	$500	$20	25.00
Feb. 1	$500	$25	20.00
March 1	$500	$15	33.33
April 1	$500	$17	29.41
May 1	$500	$25	20.00
Total	$2,500		127.74

With DCA, the gain on May 1 is $693.50 ((127.74 shares x $25/share) -$2,500). If all the shares had been purchased at $20 on January 1, the gain would have been $635 (($2,500/$20 x $25)-$2,500).

Dollar Cost Averaging Applied to the Great Depression
A study of $100 per month invested in the stock market from April 1929 to July 1934 is insightful.

Total amount invested	$6,400.00
Value at end of period	$6,545.80
Dividends	$611.50
Total value of investment	$7,157.30

The point of dollar cost averaging is that by regularly and consistently investing, risk will be minimized and consistent returns are likely to result.

Predicting the Market Direction

Market timing strategies are investment buying or selling decisions based on a predetermined catalyst. The market timer may decide in advance to sell all of his or her common stock when the Dow Jones Industrial Average reaches 3500. Establishing a purchasing or selling plan in advance is good. Advisors who propose to have the key market timing strategy should be looked upon with caution. Many timing strategies are sophisticated guesses and nothing more.

Technical and Fundamental analysis are the two primary approaches to stock market valuation. Technical analysis is based on projecting future stock prices using historical pricing information. Fundamental analysis is based on financial statements, business cycles, ratio analysis and other value-oriented indicators.

Financial ratios can help you select superior investments. The price to earnings (PE) ratio is commonly used to determine whether a stock is a good or bad buy. For instance, a stock priced at $10 per share with earnings of $1.50 has a PE ratio of 6.67.

$$\frac{\text{Price Per Share}}{\text{Earnings Per Share}} = \frac{\$10}{\$1.50} = 6.67$$

All other considerations being equal, the lower the PE ratio, the better the investment opportunity. For example, a stock with a PE ratio of 6.67 would be superior to a stock with a PE ratio of 10.

Does history repeat itself? If you answered yes, you should seriously consider stocks for medium to long range investment purposes. Stocks have been the overall winner time and time again. Imagine you invested $1 in 1925. How much do you think that dollar would be worth today, if invested in common stock, bonds and at the rate of inflation? Common stock significantly outperformed bonds and inflation over this time frame (see diagram on next page).

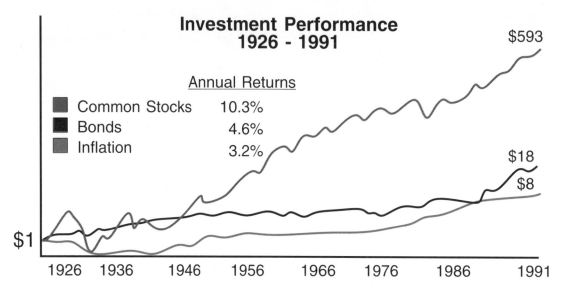

**Investment Performance
1926 - 1991**

Annual Returns
■ Common Stocks 10.3%
■ Bonds 4.6%
■ Inflation 3.2%

$593
$18
$8
$1

1926 1936 1946 1956 1966 1976 1986 1991

Source: <u>Stocks, Bonds, Bills and Inflation 1991 Yearbook</u>™,
Ibbotson Associates, Chicago.

Where most people go wrong is they buy one or two
stocks all at once. This is risky and not recommended.
Most people should not be investing at this level of risk.
Individual stocks are not suited for everyone. Consider
Strategy A, an individual stock, versus Strategy B, a
diversified portfolio. Annual deposits of $10,000 are made
and the returns below are earned.

Year	Strategy A	Strategy B
1	+16%	+8%
2	+16%	+8%
3	+16%	+8%
4	-12%	+8%
5	+16%	+8%

Surprisingly stable growth or Strategy B wins. Strategy B's growth is based on
consistent growth. Diversified portfolios or mutual funds are popular for this
reason.

Year	Strategy A	Strategy B
1	$11,600	$10,800
2	$25,056	$22,464
3	$40,665	$35,061
4	$44,585	$48,666
5	$63,319	$63,359

The secret to successful investing is consistent growth.

Mortgage Acceleration Options

Our mortgage is the largest debt most of us ever encounter. Paying off your mortgage is probably a goal you wish to achieve as soon as possible.

A mortgage acceleration plan is a strategy to make additional payments to reduce the life of your mortgage. A well-structured plan with insurance benefits provides significantly greater financial security because it will accelerate your mortgage payment at a time when you need it most. Consider the following side-by-side analysis of a prepayment plan and a mortgage protection plan:

Increased Payment Plan

1. The number of mortgage payments and interest paid is reduced. For example, making an extra payment of $4,000 a year for the first seven years on a $100,000 10% 30-year mortgage would reduce the number of years to make payments from 30 to 14.

2. A survey of homeowners who lost their homes identified a disability of the homeowner as the primary reason (49% of the time) for foreclosure. Increasing your payments will not help you, if you are sick or hurt and cannot work.

3. What if you need to make your minimum mortgage payment and you have lost access to your current income stream? The increased payment plan can expose you to the risk of not having access to the funds sent in earlier.

4. Should a terminal illness or major organ transplant be required, the home may need to be sold to generate needed funds. Unlikely, yet this severe need can destroy your financial plans.

5. Calculate the real cost of the mortgage. If you are paying 10% and inflation is averaging 6%, your inflation adjusted cost is 4%. Since mortgage interest payments are tax deductible, the deduction may be worth 3% in tax savings. Your real cost is 1%. Where can you get your hands on money for 1%?

Mortgage Protection Plan

1. The same $4,000 dropped into a mutual fund based life insurance plan could pay off the mortgage in the same amount of time or in just a few more years.

2. In the event of death, tax-free funds are available to pay the mortgage off in full.

3. Should you become sick or hurt, the mortgage protection plan can continue the premium payments, your income or both (depending on plan configuration).

4. Should a terminal illness or major organ transplant arise, you have the funds to care for yourself and even pay off your mortgage if you elect to do so.

5. Your money would grow tax-deferred and could result in a real gain compared to accumulating the funds in a separate account (see Table 3 on page 65).

6. Some states offer protection of the investment values in the event creditors try to go after your assets. Your home and this valuable program may be available for you in the worst of times.

7. The ever increasing pool of funds will serve as a source of emergency funds in the event you lose your job or just cannot make your regular mortgage payment. Whether you live, die, become disabled or just fall upon hard times, you do not have to worry about losing your home.

Five Scenarios Reviewed

A review of the following five scenarios can help you determine the value of a mortgage acceleration plan.

Scenario One

Imagine that John has worked hard and has struggled to send in his extra savings to the mortgage company for three years. John's firm decides to downsize and he loses his job. Where will the extra money come from to make the mortgage payments? If John had started a mortgage protection plan, at the end of year 3 John's plan would have sufficient cash to pay the mortgage for at least another year without worry (see Table 2).

Scenario Two

If John had been hurt instead of losing his job, what would have happened in year 3? Would the bank immediately threaten to foreclose on the home when John falls behind on his mortgage payments? A mortgage protection plan would have come to the rescue. John's mortgage payments could have been picked up by his protection plan immediately or after 60 days of disability (if configured with income replacement). At a minimum, deposits to the fund would be made and the emergency fund within the plan would cover the payment for at least another year (See Table 2).

Scenario Three

John is killed in an accident. How would John's family continue to make the payment without his support? A mortgage protection plan would instantaneously create in excess of $100,000 tax-free and John's family would not have to worry about the mortgage at all (see Table 2).

Scenario Four

At work, John sees the company doctor for a routine physical. Unfortunately, John finds out his liver is not functioning properly. The situation gets worse and John needs a new liver. John's health plan through work only provides for half of the cost of this operation. John considers selling his home to get the needed money to help pay for the operation. A mortgage protection plan could have created the funds necessary and allowed John and his family to keep their home.

Scenario Five

John sends in a deposit of $4,000 a year to his mortgage company. John continues this strategy for seven years in a row. John is fortunate and a

disability or death does not strike. Furthermore, he did not need to use an emergency fund to help make the minimum payments.

John completes paying off his mortgage in just over 14 years (Table 1). John could have obtained the peace of mind of the mortgage protection plan and still accelerated his home ownership to year 17. As time continues, the total fund for retirement (at age 65 or 30 years) or any other purpose is greater in the mortgage protection plan.

Summary

A mortgage protection plan is a better alternative for many people. The added benefits far outweigh the few additional years, if any, of mortgage payments.

A mortgage protection plan maximizes the important elements of family protection, emergency access and tax-deferred growth, while retaining your tax deduction on the interest. In the final analysis, both strategies are good, but the mortgage protection plan is usually better.

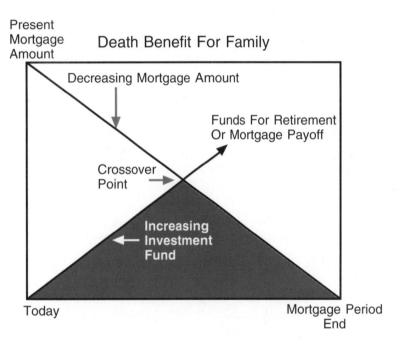

Alternative Strategies Compared

The alternative strategies are compared on next page. The effect of making additional payments of $4,000 on a $100,000 fixed mortgage at 10% is illustrated. The mortgage is paid in full in just under 15 years.

Table 1   Additional Payment Made To Mortgage Company
10% Fixed Mortgage - $877.58 Required Payment

Start of Year	Normal Mortgage Balance	The effect of a $4,000 extra payment for the first 7 years
1	$100,000	$100,000
2	$99,444	$95,062
3	$98,830	$89,607
4	$98,152	$83,580
5	$97,402	$76,922
6	$96,574	$69,568
7	$95,660	$61,443
8	$94,650	$52,467
9	$93,533	$46,934
10	$92,300	$40,822
11	$90,938	$34,069
12	$89,434	$26,609
13	$87,771	$18,368
14	$85,935	$9,265
15	$83,906	($792)
		Paid in full

The mortgage prepayment strategy helped this person pay off the mortgage in less than half the time. Table 2 reflects the impact the extra $4,000 would have had in a mortgage protection plan.

Table 2   Insurance Mortgage Protection Plan
(Male, Select, Preferred, Age 35, 9.5% consistent return)

Year	Normal Payment Balance	Principal And Interest To Be Paid	Interest Savings When Paid In Advance	Investment Accumulation Fund
1	$100,000	$315,925	$215,925	$2,888
2	$99,444	$305,394	$205,950	$7,044
3	$98,830	$294,863	$196,033	$11,584
4	$98,152	$284,333	$186,181	$16,544
5	$97,402	$273,802	$176,400	$21,963
6	$96,574	$263,271	$166,697	$28,117
7	$95,660	$252,740	$157,080	$34,823
8	$94,650	$242,210	$147,560	$37,904
9	$93,533	$231,678	$138,145	$41,244
10	$92,300	$221,147	$128,847	$44,864
11	$90,938	$210,617	$119,679	$48,607
12	$89,434	$200,087	$110,653	$52,673
13	$87,771	$189,555	$101,784	$57,084
14	$85,935	$179,025	$93,090	$61,870
15	$83,906	$168,494	$84,588	$67,061
16	$81,665	$157,963	$76,298	$73,303
17	**$79,189**	$147,432	$68,243	**$80,092**

The investment accumulation exceeds the outstanding loan in year 17.

Should death strike, the family receives the investment accumulation and the amount at risk tax-free (see Chapter 5).

Example:
In this example, John earns 9.5% in both the taxable and tax-favored account. John's tax on investment earnings is a constant 28%. John has a 30-year fixed mortgage at 10%. In order to retain his tax deduction, John decides not to prepay his 30-year mortgage. The extra $4,000 for seven years remained in a CD account and was not touched for mortgage payments. The same amount remained in the insurance account and likewise remained untouched.

Table 3 The Accumulation Power of Investment Insurance
(Male, Select, Non-Smoker, $100,000 death benefit, Age 35, 9.5% consistent return)

Year	CD Fund	Insurance Fund	Year	CD Fund	Insurance Fund
1	$4,274	$2,888	16	$66,757	$73,303
2	$8,840	$7,044	17	$71,323	$80,092
3	$13,718	$11,584	18	$76,201	$87,475
4	$18,930	$16,544	19	$81,413	$95,501
5	$24,498	$21,963	20	$86,982	$104,224
6	$30,447	$28,117	21	$92,932	$113,794
7	$36,803	$34,823	22	$99,288	$124,287
8	$39,321	$37,904	23	$106,079	$135,782
9	$42,010	$41,244	24	$113,335	$148,357
10	$44,884	$44,864	25	$121,087	$162,092
11	$47,954	$48,607	26	$129,370	$176,819
12	$51,234	$52,673	27	$138,219	$192,858
13	$54,738	$57,084	28	$147,673	$210,315
14	$58,483	$61,870	29	$157,774	$229,304
15	$62,483	$67,061	30	$168,565	$249,934

Taxes on the CD exceed the insurance cost on the mortgage protection plan, assuming a constant 9.5% return. The mortgage protection plan would net an additional $81,369 for John.

An exact analysis requires the actual tax deduction saving, mortgage interest rate and investment return. The next step requires projecting your net investment return and your mortgage interest rate.

Final Analysis
(Both Accounts Earn 9.5%)

	CD Taxable Account	**Insurance Fund** Tax-Favored
John's Age 65	$168,565	$249,934

John benefits from both tremendous protection and greater investment accumulation in the insurance fund.

Consult a qualified financial consultant if you think a mortgage acceleration plan is of benefit to you.

The first day of college is an exciting and stressful time. Imagine you are standing in a long line trying to register for classes. You are wondering if you will be able to get the classes you wish to have. You are probably are also wondering whether or not you will obtain good grades. The campus is huge and you are hoping to find your way around. This is the first time you have been away from home. You have a lot on your mind.

Hopefully, the one thing you aren't worrying about is whether your family has enough money to pay your tuition.

The Cost of College

Sending your child to college is usually very expensive. Getting an early start can help reduce the burden. You should plan on tuition, fees, and living expenses to range from $5,000 a year to $28,000 a year. Total costs at a state school may equal $5,000. You could reduce the $5,000 figure to $3,500 if your child lives at home. You may want your child to attend M.I.T. or Harvard. A top private school may range from $19,000 to $28,000 per year in today's dollars.

Years	Inflation Factor 5%
1	1.05
2	1.10
3	1.16
4	1.22
5	1.28
6	1.34
7	1.41
8	1.48
9	1.55
10	1.63
11	1.71
12	1.80
13	1.89
14	1.98
15	2.08
16	2.18
17	2.29
18	2.41
19	2.53
20	2.65
21	2.79
22	2.93

Calculate the cost of college by entering the factors from the table on the previous page.

$_____ x_____ = $_____
(first year annual cost)   (factor)   (adjusted annual cost)

$_____ x_____ = $_____
(second year annual cost)   (factor)   (adjusted annual cost)

$_____ x_____ = $_____
(third year annual cost)   (factor)   (adjusted annual cost)

$_____ x_____ = $_____
(fourth year annual cost)   (factor)   (adjusted annual cost)

Total the first through the fourth year of college. = $_____

Example: Megan is eight years old. Her parents would like to send her to a good public college averaging $10,000 per year today. How much will the $10,000 increase if inflation is 5% per year for the next 10 years? Applying the formula on the previous page, the first year adjusted annual cost equals $16,300. The total cost for four years equals $70,300 ($16,300 + $17,100 + $18,000 + $18,900).

The Six Perspectives Applied

A college funding program is like many other financial challenges. That is, you should apply the six perspectives of financial planning. Remember, this concept is based on the premise that your financial plan is only as strong as the weakest link. The six perspectives of financial planning can help you focus on your financial goals. Consequently, the following six perspectives will help you ensure a rock solid financial plan.

1. If I live, is my college funding plan based on sound principles?
2. If I become disabled or die, will my child still go to college?
3. Are the funds for college protected from lawsuits?
4. Does my college funding plan minimize the effect of taxes?
5. What happens to my college funding plan in an emergency?
6. After I send my child to college, will my plan help me provide for a secure retirement?

Most people only think of wealth accumulation when they plan for college funding. The point made by the six perspectives is simple. A good college plan will send your child to college, regardless of whether you are healthy, disabled, bankrupt, terminally ill or have died.

Sound Principles

Since the actual accumulation date is beyond five years, you should seriously consider equities for this accumulation goal (see Chapter 6). A sound principle is that stocks outperform bonds and inflation for long-term goals. Refer to the diagram on page 60. If you wish less investment risk, you may decide to add a mix of bonds.

Zero Coupon Bonds are purchased at a discount and mature at their face value. Zeros are conservative investments if held to maturity. Zeros pay no interest until they mature. This is an advantage if you wish to leave the income in the investment. Normally, leaving the income untouched is ideal for college funding. However, zeros can fluctuate a significant amount if not held to maturity. Be aware of the fact that Zeros create phantom income each year prior to maturity.

U.S. Savings bonds (EE Series) have tax advantages for some investors. Series EE bonds are backed by the U.S. government and are very safe. The interest on EE bonds is exempt from state and local taxes. Interest on EE bonds is paid upon redemption. For qualified investors, Series EE bonds may be redeemed tax free if the funds are used to pay for a child's college expenses. In order to qualify, married couples must have adjusted gross incomes of $66,700 a year or under; single people must have incomes of $44,500 or under. A proportionate scale applies to people with income in excess of the limit.

Your child may be able to help pay for some of the costs of college through part-time work. It is unrealistic, however, to expect your child to be able to pay for the entire cost of college through part-time work. Most people who work full-time do not earn $28,000 per year after taxes. A scholarship can be of great help. The problem with scholarships is you can't plan on receiving one. Don't count on unknowns when you plan your future finances.

Borrowing against the value of your home to send your child to college is a risky strategy. You can lose your home if you fall upon hard times. Furthermore, starting a new mortgage just as you are about to reach your retirement years is extremely depressing. If you have to rely on this strategy, at least you may have tax benefits from the home equity loan (see Chapter 3).

Investment insurance is an ideal part of a college funding program. Consider investment based life insurance to help meet your future accumulation needs. Often, a zero coupon bond fund within the insurance plan is an ideal selection for 25% to 50% of your investment configuration for college planning. The tax advantages discussed in Chapter 5 deserve serious consideration.

Disability or Death Protection

A superior college funding plan remains intact should you become disabled. You should have adequate coverage to replace your current income. If you do not, circle this crutch and talk to your financial consultant.

If you choose an Ivy League school at $28,000 per year, you would need $63,052 in life insurance today to guarantee this child will go to college. Taking interest of 8% and inflation of 5% into account, the $63,052 would grow to the $370,603 that will be needed in the future.

An exceptional plan would provide benefits if terminally ill or a need for a major organ transplant occurs. Modern life insurance policies provide funds for major organ transplants.

Creditor Protection

Some states specifically exempt life insurance and its investment values as creditor proof. This exemption even applies to investment heavy life insurance plans. Consult with your financial consultant about asset protection techniques.

Minimizing Taxes

Many people buy annuities for college funding. Annuities are unsuitable in most situations, due to the 10% penalty tax on premature distributions (see Chapter 9). Investment-based life insurance is a preferred vehicle, due to its tax-free access of funds (see Chapter 5).

Emergency Access

The ultimate emergencies were covered in perspective number two. A routine emergency might be an immediate need for $500. Say for instance, your car breaks down. Would your financial plan fall apart? A good plan will provide for access to funds in an emergency. Investment life insurance plans allow for emergency access to funds in denominations as low as $500.

Will My Plan Help Me After My Child Finishes School?

A good plan continues to grow even after your child has finished college. An investment life insurance plan can provide benefits for many years to come. The accelerated benefit provision (see Chapter 5) provides funds for permanent nursing home care. The tax advantages of the plan continue into the future.

College Funding Summary

Learning to think in terms of the six perspectives is the responsible thing to do. The ideal plan will most likely consist of equity-based mutual funds and might include a mix of bonds. Insurance can help turn a shaky plan into a solid plan. The bottom line is a good college funding plan will guarantee that your child goes to college.

Increased life expectancies have resulted in retirements that may last 30 or more years. A successful retirement plan will allow you to travel, pursue other interests and maintain your standard of living. To construct a sound retirement plan, think of retirement planning in terms of pre-retirement and post-retirement periods of time.

Pre-Retirement

Pre-retirement includes the actions you take during your working years to accumulate the funds you will need the day you retire. The first step is to decide how much money you will need to retire comfortably.

Retirement Calculation

1. Determine the percent of your current income you will need.

$\underline{\hspace{3cm}}$ x $\underline{\hspace{1.5cm}}$% = $\underline{\hspace{4cm}}$
(current income)   (e.g., 70%)   (income needed)

2. Project your income from other sources at retirement.

Estimate annual pension benefits (your pension administrator at work can help you with this estimate):

$\underline{\hspace{3cm}}$

Estimate annual Social Security income (this information is on your Social Security verification form, see page 73): $\underline{\hspace{3cm}}$

Retirement savings to date: $\underline{\hspace{3cm}}$

3. Adjust numbers from 1 and 2 to accurately reflect the impact of 5% inflation.

Years to retirement	10	15	20	25
Inflation factors (5%)	1.63	2.08	2.65	3.39

$\underline{\hspace{3cm}}$ x $\underline{\hspace{1cm}}$ = $\underline{\hspace{4cm}}$
(income needed)   (factor)   (adjusted income needed)

$\underline{\hspace{3cm}}$ x $\underline{\hspace{1cm}}$ = $\underline{\hspace{4cm}}$
(pension)   (factor)   (adjusted pension)

$\underline{\hspace{3cm}}$ x $\underline{\hspace{1cm}}$ = $\underline{\hspace{4cm}}$
(Social Security)   (factor)   (adjusted Social Security)

4. Subtract the adjusted pension and adjusted Social Security from the adjusted income needed.

$_____ - $_____ = $_____
    (adjusted income   (adjusted pension   (annual shortfall)
        needed)   and adjusted
                    Social Security)

Annual shortfall divided by 12 = $_____
                                (monthly shortfall)

5. The following table illustrates how much you will need in order to generate $100 in monthly income for various lengths of time.

	Annual rate of return		
Years in retirement	8%	10%	12%
10 years	$8,397	$7,767	$7,213
15 years	$10,711	$9,614	$8,695
20 years	$12,286	$10,762	$9,536
25 years	$13,358	$11,474	$10,013

$_____ x $_____ = $_____
  (amount from table)   (shortfall divided by 100)   (preliminary goal)

Example: Assume your monthly shortfall is $2,000 and you want income to continue for 20 years. You anticipate a 10% rate of return. The intersection of 20 years and 10% is $10,762. Multiply $10,762 by 20 (your shortfall divided by 100). Your preliminary retirement goal equals $215,240.

6. The preliminary goal must be increased to account for inflation. A factor of 1.5 (conservative) to 2.0 (very conservative) will provide you with a rough estimate.

$_____ x _____ = $_____
  (preliminary goal)   (factor 1.5 to 2.0)   (retirement goal)

7. The next step is to adjust current savings for the growth that you expect to occur between now and the day you retire.

	Annual rate of return		
Years to retirement	8%	10%	12%
10 years	2.16	2.59	3.11
15 years	3.17	4.18	5.47
20 years	4.66	6.73	9.65
25 years	6.85	10.83	17.00

$_____ x _____ = $_____
  (current savings)   (factor)   (projected savings)

8. Determine your retirement gap by subtracting from your retirement goal the projected value of your savings calculated in step seven. A negative number means you are already in position to attain your goal.

$_____ - $_____ = $_____
  (retirement goal)   (projected savings)   (retirement gap)

9. Now that you know what you will need, calculate how much you need to save each year to fill the gap.

	Annual rate of return		
Years to retirement	**8%**	**10%**	**12%**
10 years	.0690	.0627	.0570
15 years	.0368	.0315	.0268
20 years	.0219	.0175	.0139
25 years	.0137	.0102	.0075

$_____ x _____ = $_____
  (retirement gap)   (factor)   (annual savings needed)

Divide your annual savings needed by 12 to determine the amount each month you need to save.

$_____ divided by 12 = $_____
  (annual amount)   (monthly savings needed)

The Three Legs of Retirement Income

Imagine that on the day you retire, you are going to sit on a chair with three legs. These three legs will be your "pillars of stability" for the years to come. These legs are:

1. Social Security.
2. Employer-sponsored plans.
3. Individual plans.

Let's examine each leg of retirement income.

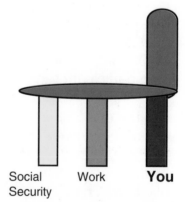

Social Security   Work   **You**

Social Security

Every two or three years, you should request your earnings and benefit estimate summary. The Social Security Administration will send you Form SSA-7004-PC-OP3, which will allow you to receive retirement, survivor and disability income benefit estimates. You should factor in your expected benefits, but also realize that a heavy strain exists on the Social Security Administration.

Your primary purpose in requesting your benefit estimate is to ensure that your income and taxes paid are correctly recorded. The Social Security Administration admits a 7.7% error factor. If you do find an error, you need to send a copy of the disputed year's tax records to the Social Security Administration.

Employer-Sponsored Plans

Employer-sponsored plans or qualified retirement plans are ideal for a portion of your retirement funds. There are two major classifications of qualified retirement plans. The first is a defined benefit plan. That is, the retirement benefit is a definitely defined amount. The second is a defined contribution plan. A defined contribution plan has a known contribution, but an unknown retirement benefit. A defined contribution plan places the investment risk and reward with the employee. Defined contribution plans are more popular due to less employer risk and administrative expense.

If your employer matches your contribution to a qualified plan, you should always contribute at least the minimum amount required to qualify for the match. The inherent systematic savings feature of qualified plans is a substantial benefit. Many people find the bulk of their funds for retirement have been saved in qualified retirement plans.

SEPPs

Simplified Employee Pension Plans (SEPP) are very similar to Individual Retirement Accounts. SEPPs are ideal for people involved in a professional practice or small business. An employer can contribute and deduct up to 15% of covered payroll. Contributions accumulate tax-deferred and are subject to a 10% penalty tax if withdrawn prior to age 59½. Firms with less than 25 employees can also allow participants to make voluntary pre-tax salary deferrals of up to $8,728 (1992) or 15% of compensation, if less, each year. The total allocated to any plan participant cannot exceed the lesser of 15% of compensation or $30,000.

Operating a SEPP is simple and cost effective. All employees must participate, except employees under 21 years of age, employees who earn less than $300 per year from the employer, and those employees who have not performed any work for you in three of the last five years. Other exceptions include nonresident aliens with no U.S. earned income and union employees, if retirement benefits have been subject to good faith collective bargaining.

Will your retirement income be cut in half?

The Hidden Risk of Qualified Retirement Plans

Qualified retirement plans are an excellent component of a retirement accumulation plan. A hidden risk of qualified retirement plans is that your spendable income will be exposed to the tax rates in effect at retirement.

74

The question of future taxes is especially important to consider when funding a qualified retirement plan. To gain a better understanding of this hidden risk, examine the impact of taxes in the future with two different effective tax rates. The qualified retirement plan in this example will generate $50,000 per year in income for twenty years.

Pay Tax on Retirement Income	Pay Tax on Retirement Income
Retirement Income $50,000	Retirement Income $50,000
If taxed at 31%, then tax equals $15,500	If taxed at 50%, then tax equals $25,000
Years of Income 20	Years of Income 20
Total Taxes $310,000	Total Taxes $500,000

Even after factoring in the time value of money, you may be able to increase your total income received with a prepay tax strategy.

You must be very careful when taking distributions from your retirement plan. If you take too much too early, or too little too late, it can be costly. The following taxes under current tax laws may apply to your qualified retirement distribution:

During Life:
Early Distribution Penalty	10%
Excess Distribution Penalty	15%
Delayed Distribution Penalty	50%
Federal Income Tax	31%

After Death:
Excess Accumulation Penalty	15%
Income in Respect of a Decedent Tax	31%
Federal Estate Tax	50%

When you add up the effect of taxes, you may find the net to your heirs is less than 22%.

Individual Plans
IRAs
An Individual Retirement Account (IRA) provides a current year tax deduction and is easy to maintain. The Tax Reform Act of 1986 restricted the IRA deduction for participants in other qualified retirement plans. The maximum contribution is $2,000 per individual and $2,250 for a spousal IRA. IRAs are similar to qualified retirement plans in that certain distributions prior to age 59½ are taxed with an additional 10% penalty tax.

IRA Deduction Table (assuming active participation in a qualified retirement plan)

Joint Taxpayer Returns

Adjusted Gross Income	IRA Deduction If One Spouse Has An IRA	IRA Deduction For Two IRAs	IRA Deduction For Spousal IRA
$40,000 and under	$2,000	$4,000	$2,250
$41,000	$1,800	$3,600	$2,025
$42,000	$1,600	$3,200	$1,800
$43,000	$1,400	$2,800	$1,575
$44,000	$1,200	$2,400	$1,350
$45,000	$1,000	$2,000	$1,125
$46,000	$800	$1,600	$900
$47,000	$600	$1,200	$675
$48,000	$400	$800	$450
$49,000	$200	$400	$225
$50,000	$0	$0	$0

For married couples, if either spouse is an active participant, then both husband and wife are considered active participants.

Single Taxpayer Returns

Adjusted Gross Income	IRA Deduction
$25,000 and under	$2,000
$26,000	$1,800
$27,000	$1,600
$28,000	$1,400
$29,000	$1,200
$30,000	$1,000
$31,000	$800
$32,000	$600
$33,000	$400
$34,000	$200
$35,000	$0

Example: Steve is single and an active participant in his employer's qualified retirement plan. Steve's adjusted gross income is $30,000 and, therefore, Steve may make a deductible IRA contribution of $1,000.

The Internal Revenue Code Section 219 (g)(2)(B) allows for a minimum deduction of $200 for married couples with incomes under $50,000 or single people under $35,000.

Private Pension Plans
The tax advantages of private pension plans make them excellent complements to employer-sponsored retirement plans. The family protection component provides guarantees unmatched by qualified plans, IRAs or other retirement plans.

A private pension plan may generate greater income during retirement due to the fact that tax-free distributions are allowed. The strategy is to withdraw the amount contributed tax free, then borrow the gain tax free. Properly structured, the loan is repaid at death by the tax-free death benefit. Lifetime tax avoidance is achieved immediately after the deposit is made.

Distributions in the form of withdrawals and loans should never exceed the amount needed to maintain the life insurance protection. Should the life insurance protection discontinue, the amount by which total loans and withdrawals exceeds the total deposits made to the plan would be exposed to taxation. A knowledgeable financial consultant can assist you and provide annual updates on the progress of your private pension plan.

The following side-by-side comparison of a private pension plan and qualified retirement plan is particularly useful in helping you understand why many people feel it is important to fund both plans.

Qualified Retirement Plan

Advantages:
- ♦ Deposits are tax deductible.
- ♦ Assets accumulate tax deferred.

Disadvantages:
- ♦ Retirement income is taxable (possibly at a higher rate).
- ♦ Excess distribution subject to additional excise tax.
- ♦ Pre-retirement death benefit may be taxable.
- ♦ Post-retirement death benefit is taxable.
- ♦ Contributions limited by law.
- ♦ IRS approval required.
- ♦ Funds may not be available prior to retirement without penalty (age 59½), and systematic liquidation must begin by 70½.
- ♦ Plan termination requires IRS approval.
- ♦ Not self-completing in the event of disability.
- ♦ No accelerated benefits for a terminal illness or permanent confinement to a nursing home.

Private Pension Plan

Advantages:
- ♦ Assets accumulate tax deferred.
- ♦ Retirement income is tax free.
- ♦ Contributions and benefits are not limited by law.
- ♦ IRS approval not required.
- ♦ Borrowing allowed without restriction.
- ♦ Withdrawal of funds available before age 59½ without tax penalty--with no limit as to when liquidation must begin.
- ♦ No trust or trustee required.
- ♦ May be self-completing in the event of disability.
- ♦ May provide protection for a terminal illness or permanent confinement to a nursing home.
- ♦ Attractive, guaranteed fixed-interest returns available.
- ♦ Portable, travels with you all the time.
- ♦ Pre-retirement death benefit is tax free.
- ♦ Post-retirement death benefit is tax free.
- ♦ Passes to beneficiaries outside of probate.

Disadvantages:
- ♦ Deposits are not tax deductible.
- ♦ Termination of the plan exposes the gain to income taxes.

The private pension plan is often the perfect supplement to a qualified retirement plan. Due to the insurance benefits provided, the private pension plan is more efficient at younger ages. People in poor health or who are age 50 or older may need to consider supplementing their plans at work with an annuity. A knowledgeable financial consultant can provide you with a cost-benefit analysis of your situation.

A well-designed plan will be in compliance with current tax laws. If structured incorrectly, a modified endowment contract may result. A modified endowment contract is taxed in a manner similar to other tax-deferred vehicles. Refer to pages 36 to 40 for quantitative analysis. Since the availability of these plans is relatively recent, consider the following common questions and answers.

Q. *What is the private pension plan?*
A. It is a tax-favored strategy of accumulating funds for retirement.

Q. *What are the tax advantages?*
A. Tax-deferred accumulations on earnings and tax-free withdrawals.

Q. *Are the funds restricted to retirement?*
A. No. The plan allows for access to cash for emergencies, college funding, mortgage acceleration and any other reason.

Q. *What is the penalty for early withdrawal?*
A. None. Unlike qualified plans, there is no 10% penalty for early withdrawals.

Q. *How is that possible?*
A. The funding vehicle used is a low-cost life insurance contract, wrapped in various investment portfolios.

Q. *How can life insurance be an investment?*
A. Under current IRS Code Section 7702, accumulations in life insurance contracts grow tax deferred. By using a low-cost life contract and combining it with various investment options, the tax advantages of life insurance and performance of mutual funds is achieved.

Q. *How can tax avoidance be maintained after death?*
A. The use of the death benefit to repay a loan does not cause the recognition of taxable income. As a general rule, death proceeds are excludable from a beneficiary's gross income (IRS Code Section 101(a)(1)).

Q. *What about the investment options?*
A. You select mutual funds based upon your investment objectives and risk tolerance.

Q. *What if my health changes after I have started participation?*
A. A private pension plan is irrevocably based on your health at the time of plan inception.

Q. *What if tax laws change after I start my plan?*
A. Tax laws are constantly changing. Fortunately, a precedent has been established for similar plans. The concept is referred to as grandfathering. Under the grandfathering concept, tax law changes do not adversely affect plans already inforce. The private pension plan you start today will more than likely continue to be treated under the tax laws in effect the day you started your plan.

The flexibility of a private pension plan is remarkable. Consider how a private pension plan can help you both today and tomorrow.

Plan Benefits	Plan Tackles These Obstacles
Accumulates Wealth	Taxes
Has Dollar Cost Averaging	Bad Investments
Offers Systematic Saving	Procrastination
Offers Mutual Funds	Inadequate Diversification
Solid Family Protection	Death or Disability
Sound Mortgage Acceleration	Medical Expenses
Helps With College Funding	Inflation
Completely Portable	Termination of Employment
May Offer Creditor Protection*	Lawsuits or Property Loss
Pays For Nursing Home Care	Risk of Outliving Funds

*State-to-state creditor protection ranges from none to 100%.

The private pension plan may also help solve estate, charitable giving, executive compensation or pension maximization financial goals. A knowledgeable financial consultant can design a personalized private pension plan for you.

Annuities

An annuity is an investment purchased from a life insurance company that accumulates wealth tax deferred under Section 72 of the Internal Revenue Code. The power of tax-deferred growth can be a tremendous benefit. Consider the following growth of a taxable and a tax-deferred account.

Example: A $100 a week deposit into an investment earning 11.11% (28% tax-bracket).

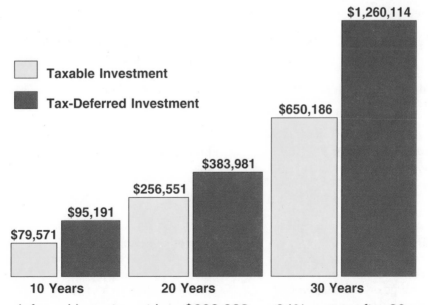

The tax-deferred investment has $609,928, or 94%, more after 30 years.

Annuities are often an excellent vehicle to meet your needs during retirement. Annuities offer guaranteed fixed investments, as well as mutual fund investments. The owner of an annuity also has the option of taking monthly income over a fixed number of years or over a person's lifetime. There is no limit as to the amount of money that can be deposited in an annuity. The tax-favored treatment of annuities often make them ideal components of a solid retirement plan.

Annuities can be mysterious to the average investor. Annuities are actually easy to understand and offer a number of unique benefits. Another way of understanding annuities is to think of life insurance in reverse. Annuities provide a flow of income you can never outlive. Options for income are numerous, and can be tailored for your specific need.

Consider this comparison between an annuity and a Certificate of Deposit to better understand an annuity's benefits.

Certificate of Deposit	Annuity
Safety: A bank CD offers guaranteed principal and interest up to $100,000.	**Safety:** A fixed annuity offers guaranteed principal and interest beyond $100,000.
Bypass Probate: No.	**Bypass Probate:** Yes.
Every Dollar At Work (No Front Load): Yes. Invest $10,000 and $10,000 is in your account.	**Every Dollar At Work (No Front Load):** Yes. Invest $10,000 and $10,100 is in your account (1% bonus is normal).
Tax-Deferred Growth: No. Each year IRS-1099 issued.	**Tax-Deferred Growth:** Yes. Can defer up to age 100.
Social Security Tax Relief: No.	**Social Security Tax Relief:** Yes, if structured properly.
Guaranteed Lifetime Tax-Advantaged Income Provision: No.	**Guaranteed Lifetime Tax-Advantaged Income Provision:** Yes.
Liquidity (Access To Funds): Seven days upon maturity. For instance, a one-year CD provides a total of twenty-eight days or one month every four years (7 x 4) of access without penalties.	**Liquidity (Access To Funds):** Allows for 10% free withdrawals after the first year. Immediate income annuities provide immediate income without penalty charge.
Surrender charge: Six months' interest whether earned or not is a common penalty for early surrender of a CD. Surrender charge on a $100,000 CD earning 9% is depicted by diagram A.	**Surrender charge:** Decreasing schedule eventually vanishing after seven or eight years. Typical surrender charge for a $100,000 annuity earning 9% is depicted by diagram B.

Diagram A (Certificate of Deposit):

Surrender Charge	$4500	$4905	$5346	$5827	$6352	$6923	$7546	$8226
Year	1	2	3	4	5	6	7	8

Diagram B (Annuity):

Surrender Charge	$5886	$5346	$4662	$3811	$2541	$1509	$0	$0
Year	1	2	3	4	5	6	7	8

When a closer look is applied to these two alternatives, it is easy to see why an annuity often is the preferred choice for accumulation goals.

The Legal Reserve System

The Legal Reserve System was established in 1906 and requires insurance companies to maintain specific levels of assets to support liabilities. These assets consist of cash values, reserves and surplus. Insurance companies are monitored closely and investment selection for these assets is regulated by law.

The Hidden Risk In Annuity Income

As discussed previously in this book, you will very likely retire to a higher tax-bracket. For a moment, imagine that nationalized health care and Social Security entitlements result in two 11% increases (total of 22%) to the Federal Income Tax rates. You currently pay tax at the 28% rate, so your future rate in this projection is now 50%. Consequently, if you need $50,000 a year during retirement, you may need to take $100,000 (if qualified), or a somewhat lower amount if not qualified, out of your annuity. This is called the IOU effect with annuities. You owe Uncle Sam taxes based on rates to be determined in the future. Annuities lose a lot of their appeal during the payout phase if income tax rates are higher.

Post-Retirement

The day you stop working, you start the post-retirement phase. The average retiree spends about 18 years in this phase. Special planning considerations apply to post-retirement.

A common post-retirement fallacy is that your tax rate will be lower the day you retire. If you plan to retire with the same income you have today, why would your future tax rate be lower? If there is any change, a strong argument for a higher tax rate can be found in Chapter 1. The sad reality is that many people really do retire to a lower tax rate. Unfortunately, this is because these people failed to plan for the future and live in poverty, or well below their desired standard of living.

Your investment portfolio may need to be positioned with less risk. A bad investment is harder to overcome, since you are no longer working. Nonetheless, a portfolio of guaranteed investments only will result in a reduction in buying power. A real danger of outliving your retirement income exists when you invest only in low risk investments. Positioning 25% to 50% of your investment portfolio in conservatively managed equities is often optimal. Many financial consultants agree that 15% is the minimum amount that should be invested in growth stocks. Consider investing the remaining dollars in money market funds, certificates of deposit, government bonds, corporate bonds, municipal bonds, government securities, annuities and single premium life contracts.

Single premium life contracts offer substantial benefits for a retiree. Some of the benefits offered by a superior plan may surprise you. The first is that the accelerated death benefit can help pay for nursing home care or a major organ transplant operation. The second is that the contract grows tax-favored and usually guarantees competitive returns. Often, the tax-deferred growth results in greater investment accumulation than a current CD investment. The third benefit is that many contracts offer a one-year free look provision. The full premium is refunded if you decide to change your mind. The fourth benefit is an attractive loan feature. Many contracts allow you to withdraw funds at ½% loan interest per year. The other point to remember is the accumulation escapes all taxation if passed in the form of the death benefit. In summary, a single pay life policy offers a tremendous amount of benefits for many retirees beyond maximizing tax-free transfer of wealth. Remember, the only person that can take care of the older person you will one day be, is the younger working person you are today.

Summary

Most people need to take full advantage of employer-sponsored retirement plans. Qualified retirement plans are excellent for what they are intended to do-- provide a retirement income. The fact, however, is that even with an employer-provided plan, very few people will be able to maintain their desired standard of living after retirement without other sources of income. The Perfect Money Plan would include a private pension plan for many people. The private pension plan is an extremely flexible, attractive way to provide another source of retirement income, while addressing needs and obstacles that may arise between now and retirement in ways that can't be matched by qualified plans or other non-qualified investment plans.

Effective tax brackets tend to change significantly over time. A Perfect Money Plan will withdraw the majority of your income from taxable sources in a year when taxes are relatively low, and withdraw funds from a tax-free source in a year taxes are high.

Now you come to a very important question, "Where do you go from here?"

The answer depends on your level of sophistication. Even the experienced investor should consider the services of a professional when contemplating investment and insurance purchases. A minor mistake can set your financial plans back many years. To draw an analogy, if you had a serious medical problem, would you treat yourself or see a professional? You would no doubt seek the services of a qualified professional. Why should something as important as your financial security be any different?

The knowledge you have acquired in *Perfect Money Planning* will help you start your financial plan. In order to complete or implement your plan, you will need the services of financial professionals. Selecting financial services on a self-help basis is usually inconsistent with moderate or low risk profiles. Since many financial advisors offer initial consultations on a complimentary basis, you should consider seeking the services of financial professionals.

If you start now, you will have time and rate-of-return on your side. You will determine whether your future is happy or sad.

 or

Choosing a Financial Consultant

You have just received financial advice and immediately wonder, "Can I trust this person? The advice sounds good, but are his or her interests coming before mine? Am I paying a fair price for this investment? Could I buy it for less or at no cost? Could someone else do a better job for me? Will this strategy accomplish my goals (education funding, retirement income, etc.)? Will everything be all right?"

Investment fears are normal and should be addressed in depth. Unfortunately, the basic philosophy of many financial consultants is to only give the client the minimum information necessary to make the sale. A sound rule of thumb is that an advisor who is rushed and does not spend time before or during the sale to resolve your fears will no doubt apply the same attention to servicing your account.

Learning how to choose a financial consultant will help alleviate many of these concerns. When you are unsure, you need to ask direct questions and get direct answers. When you ask yourself if everything will be all right, you should be able to answer yes. The following checklist will assist you in making a good decision when selecting your financial consultant.

Does the person have:

	Yes	No	?
Experience?			
A commitment to professional education?			
Professional liability coverage ($1,000,000 at a minimum)?			
Needed specialty knowledge or skills?			
Ability to represent the top company?			
Solid service system?			
Personality match with you and your spouse?			
References?			

Good news. If your financial consultant does not measure up in every category, virtually every company will allow you to change representatives in order to preserve your account. One way to contact a professional in your area is to call the certifying authority for Chartered Financial Consultants and Chartered Life Underwriters, The American Society of ChFC & CLU, at 215-526-2500. The American Society will be happy to send you a free copy of "The Consumers' Guide to Insurance and Financial Services."

Compensation

Understanding how your financial consultant is compensated is important and should be discussed. Many good consultants will prepare your initial analysis and recommendations on a complimentary basis in order to earn the right to be the person you choose for financial services. A financial consultant with this perspective is in the financial services business for the long run and understands the value of client service.

Fee-based planners are paid a set amount and do not participate in receiving commissions. Fee-based planners will refer you to someone else who will receive the commission. The objectivity is great, but you end up paying considerably more for this service.

Commission-based and fee-based planning services are both sound compensation methods. You should ask your financial consultant about marketing charges, fees for planning and any additional charges that apply to servicing your plan or account.

Choosing a Financial Service Company

Selecting the right company is extremely important. Insurance purchases are especially unique and require additional care, because they usually involve extremely long-term commitments. Selecting an insurance company requires due diligence. This is due to the fact that a financial disaster can result from deficient protection plans. If an insurance company fails, most states offer limited safety nets to prevent policyholders from losing everything.

You should place your new business with financial service companies receiving solid ratings from A.M. Best (see chart on page 86). Excellent or superior ratings from Moody's and Standard & Poor's rating services are also important indicators. If your current company does not have a strong rating, seek the advice of a financial consultant.

Remember, you are usually best off keeping permanent insurance plans, even with a "middle of the road" company. Never drop permanent insurance coverage without a second opinion and a specific written year-to-year analysis. If you decide that moving from one company to another is best, take advantage of Section 1035 of the Internal Revenue Code. Section 1035 allows the tax-free exchange of one insurance policy to another insurance policy or annuity.

Partial transfers from insurance companies in conservatorship under Section 1035 have recently been allowed by the IRS (Revenue Ruling 92-43 published in IRB 1992-24, June 15, 1992). All cash received must be reinvested in the new insurance contract within 90 days of distribution. The services of a qualified Chartered Life Underwriter (CLU) or Chartered Financial Consultant (ChFC) cannot be exaggerated if you are attempting a Section 1035 exchange. A Certified Public Accountant (CPA) knowledgeable in insurance taxation is also a tremendous resource. You must consider all the ramifications pertinent to your situation.

The following checklist will help you evaluate your current or future financial service companies.

Does the company have:

	Yes	No	?
Long history of solid service?			
Nearby locations for help or service?			
An **B+** or higher financial rating from A.M. Best, if insurance?			
Assets in excess of $20 billion dollars?			
AIDS reserve, if life insurance?			
Reasonably priced products?			

If you cannot answer all of these questions, you need to take time out and do your homework. Insurance companies are regulated by each state and you can gain valuable information, such as the company's history of servicing clients, by calling your Insurance Commissioner. One "no" answer is serious enough for you to begin to investigate another alternative. Do not make the all-too-often fatal mistake of simply choosing the cheapest coverage.

The insurance industry is significantly stronger than the banking system. The reason for this strength is a longer overall investment horizon, strict regulation, conservative positioning and solid diversification. FDIC protection for the banking industry is certainly a good safety net, but so are the safety nets for insurance companies offered by most states.

Most libraries have a copy of *Best's Insurance Reports*. You can also call A.M. Best at 908-439-2200, ext. 5742. The following chart will help you translate A.M. Best symbols:

Rating	Which means
A++ or A+	Superior
A or A-	Excellent
B++ or B+	Very Good
B or B-	Good
C++ or C+	Fair
C and C-	Marginal
D	Below Minimum Standard
E	Under State Supervision
F	In Liquidation

Understanding how your financial service company plans to make a profit is important. Your financial consultant should be able to clearly explain the incentives available to the companies offering products you are considering. Always ask your financial consultant how the company can guarantee a certain return. Interest rates which sound too good to be true are almost always exactly that.

Conclusion

There is more to life than money. Nonetheless, it is only prudent to take steps to ensure financial security for yourself and the people you love. Hopefully, you have enjoyed the exercises in this book and learned more about financial planning. Transfer your work in the chapters to the appendix and you will have a concise financial plan. Remember, a good plan without the proper financial vehicles to make it work is only a piece of paper. Get off to a running start and contact your financial consultant today. Good luck and much success with your financial plan.

Date:_____

A Financial Plan For _____

Now that you have read the book, completing your financial plan is as easy as 1-2-3.

Step 1 - Financial Organization

Determine your cash flow and net worth with this worksheet.

Cash Flow Worksheet

Monthly income:

Your salary _____

Spouse's salary_____

Other pay _____

Dividends _____

Interest _____

Rental property_____

Social Security_____

Pension benefits_____

Annuities _____

Alimony _____

Other _____

Total monthly

income: $_____

Monthly expenses:

Mortgage or rent _____

Homeowners insurance _____

Life, health and
other insurance _____

Taxes _____

Installment purchase _____

Food _____

Home maintenance _____

Utilities and fuel _____

Clothing _____

Transportation _____

Entertainment _____

Travel/vacations _____

Clubs and organizations _____

Charity and gifts _____

Alimony _____

Miscellaneous _____

Total monthly

expenses: $_____

Income minus expenses

equals $_____

Net Worth Statement

Assets:

Savings accounts _____

Checking accounts _____

Certificates of deposit _____

U.S. Savings Bonds _____

Life insurance (cash value) _____

Annuities (cash value) _____

IRA account _____

Pension (vested interest) _____

Securities (market value) _____

Real estate (market value) _____

Business interest _____

Personal property _____

Other _____

Total assets: $_____

Liabilities

Mortgage (balance due) _____

Taxes _____

Installment loans _____

Charge account _____

Charitable pledges _____

Other _____

Total liabilities: $_____

Total assets: $_____

  minus

Total liabilities: $_____

Net worth: $_____

Based on a brief review of where you have been (net worth) and where you are going (cash flow), are you happy with your financial success? How much more would you like to save each month?

_____

_____

_____

_____

_____

Searching for names of financial professionals can be difficult. Take time now to list your financial professionals.

Title	Name	Phone Number
Accountant	_____	_____
Banker	_____	_____
Financial Consultant	_____	_____
Insurance Agent	_____	_____
Securities Broker	_____	_____
Attorney	_____	_____
Other	_____	_____

Personal Asset Inventory

Location of videotape of property is _____.

Date videotaping occurred _____.

I have not filmed my property, but have a written property schedule attached.

Your Legal Documents

Your last review with your attorney was _____.

Document	You	Your Spouse
Will	____	____
Living Will	____	____
Living Trust	____	____
Other_____	____	____

Step 2 - Setting and Prioritizing Goals

Place a check mark next to the goals that are important to you. Prioritize goals in order of their importance to you. You may wish to use a pencil for this exercise.

Important	Goal	Priority
☐	Establish an emergency fund.	_____
☐	Establish a Contingency Day on _____.	_____
☐	Protect my family financially.	_____
☐	Guaranteed income replacement if sick or hurt.	_____
☐	Have a comfortable retirement.	_____
☐	Save and invest systematically.	_____
☐	Complete a financial plan.	_____
☐	Protect my assets from the risk of a lawsuit.	_____
☐	Take advantage of tax-favored vehicles.	_____
☐	Protect my finances in the event of long-term nursing care.	_____
☐	Provide funds for my children's education.	_____
☐	Accumulate funds for _____.	_____
☐	Minimize my tax bite.	_____
☐	Avoid estate taxes.	_____
☐	Review my plan or specific program.	_____
☐	Establish health care for myself and/or family.	_____
☐	Obtain better property & casualty protection.	_____
☐	Start my own business.	_____
☐	Other _____.	_____

List your three most important goals:

1. _____

_____

2. _____

_____

3. _____

_____

Impending Changes

You need to consider significant changes that may impact the financial planning process. Check the following changes that may apply to you in the next two years.

Change	Projected Date
☐ Marriage	_____
☐ New home	_____
☐ Children	_____
☐ Sell property	_____
☐ Inheritance	_____
☐ Salary increase	_____
☐ Pay off loans	_____
☐ Go back to school	_____
☐ Bonus	_____
☐ Promotion	_____
☐ Change job	_____
☐ Lose job	_____
☐ Start business	_____
☐ Sell business	_____

Other changes you anticipate:_____

_____

_____

_____

_____

_____

Step 3 - Implementing Your Plan

Debt Management
Complete the next two exercises and quiz to obtain
a true picture of your debt.

Total Your Debt

Creditor	Payment Each Month	Total Interest Paid Last Month	Interest Rate Being Charged
1.			
2.			
3.			
4.			
5.			
6.			
7.			
8.			
9.			
10.			
11.			
12.			

Total $_____ $_____

Personal Debt Ratio (Debt to Earnings)

$$\frac{\text{Total debt each month (excluding mortgage)}}{} \div \frac{\text{After-tax income each month}}{} = \frac{\text{Debt Ratio}}{}$$

Debt Ratio Analysis

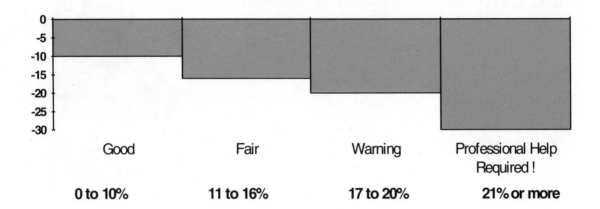

Good	Fair	Warning	Professional Help Required !
0 to 10%	**11 to 16%**	**17 to 20%**	**21% or more**

Tax Management

Circle the table that applies to your situation and take time now to projected this year's tax bill.

The standard deduction follows:

Married and Surviving Spouses	$6,200
Unmarried Individuals	$3,700
Heads of Households	$5,450
Married Filing Separate	$3,100

The personal and dependency exemption for 1993 is $2,350 for individuals.

According to the IRS, the average American works until May 8th just to pay federal, state and local taxes. Is your projected Federal Income Tax four or five months' income (including Social Security tax)?

Projecting Your Taxes

Total Annual Income (include your salary, tips, dividends, interest income, taxable Social Security and all other taxable income).

_____

Exemptions (exemptions are allowed for the taxpayer, spouse and dependents).

minus _____

Adjustments (deductible SEPP contributions and 401(k) (self-employed), IRA contributions and alimony payments).

minus _____

Adjusted Gross Income or AGI (subtract exemptions and adjustments from total annual income).

equals_____

Itemized Deductions. Actual deductions may be determined by itemizing on Schedule A. Consult your tax advisor to determine your itemized deductions and limitations that apply. The following is a brief list of expenses that are generally deductible.
- Mortgage interest
- Charitable contributions
- State and local taxes paid

equals_____

Total Taxable Income (subtract itemized deductions from adjusted gross income).

equals_____

Total Tax (refer to the tables on page 23 to calculate your tax).

equals_____

The above calculation will be an accurate projection for most taxpayers. If tax credits apply to your situation, simply reduce your total taxes due dollar for dollar. Highly compensated people should verify that no additional tax liability applies. The most common additional tax is the Alternative Minimum Tax.

Tax Strategies to Investigate

Consider discussing the following tax strategies with your financial consultant.

Tax Justice

	Yes	No
1. Prepay	_____	_____
2. Transfer	_____	_____
3. Incentive	_____	_____
4. Deferral	_____	_____
5. Deduction	_____	_____
6. Conversion	_____	_____

Insurance Management

Insurance programs help form the foundation for your family's financial security.

Calculate Your Life Insurance Need

	In the event of your death, your spouse needs?	In the event of your spouse's death, you need?
Immediate Money Fund (Medical and hospital expenses, burial expenses, attorney's fees, etc.)		
Debt Liquidation		
Emergency Fund (Unexpected needs, etc.)		
Mortgage Payment Fund		
Child/Home Care Fund		
Educational Fund		
Capital Needed To Replace Income (Divide income by rate of return; e.g., $20,000 / 8% = $250,000)*		
Subtotal		
Total Current Life Insurance		
Total Other Assets (you would like to have go toward meeting your insurance needs)		
New Capital Required (Subtract total current life insurance and other assets from subtotal)		

*To determine a more accurate value, the present value of the capital needed to replace income can be entered.

Accelerated Benefits

The accelerated benefit option, often referred to as a living needs benefit, is the biggest change in the life insurance industry since Dodson invented permanent insurance. The accelerated benefit option allows you to be your own beneficiary in the event you need a major organ transplant, are terminally ill or require permanent nursing home care.

My life insurance has accelerated benefits for: <u>Yes</u>   <u>No</u>

Major organ transplant   ____   __

Terminal illness   ____   __

Nursing home care   ____   __

Income Replacement Protection

Income continuation in the event you are sick or hurt and cannot return to work is essential. Do you have adequate coverage?

Calculate Your Disability Insurance Need

You determined your disability insurance need with the first worksheet on determining your monthly expenses.

Monthly expenses and disability insurance need equals_____.

The probability of disability is _____ (refer to graph).

Your Probability of Disability Prior To Age 65

Source: 1985 Commissioners Individual Disability A Table

Property and Casualty Coverage

Do you need to review or adjust the following policies?

	Yes or No
Auto Insurance	_____
Homeowners Insurance	_____
Umbrella Coverage	_____
Other_____	_____

Investment Management

The correct investment is an investment consistent with your risk tolerance, holding period and the erosion effect. Take time now to complete the following exercise.

Investment Selector

Investment Questions	Personal Objectives	Investment Category
What is the return you realistically require after taxes?	☐ 6% or less every year ☐ 6% to 8% every year ☐ 8% to 11% every year ☐ 11% to 15% every year ☐ 15% or more every year	Very High Safety Moderate Safety Some Risk Substantial Risk Extremely High Risk
How would you assess your risk tolerance on a scale of 1 to 9, with 1 being very conservative and 9 being very risky?	☐ 1-3 ☐ 4-5 ☐ 6-9	Safety Is Important Some Risk Substantial To Extreme Risk

If you had just won $10,000 in the lottery, which would you choose?	☐ Stocks ☐ Mutual Funds ☐ Certificate of Deposit	Substantial To Extreme Risk Some Risk Safety Is Important
What do you want your investment to do for you?	☐ Want no current income ☐ Want interest to grow ☐ Want to spend interest ☐ Want to spend principal	Growth Objective Income Objective
How do you feel about tax-favored investments?	☐ No interest ☐ Marginal interest ☐ Very important	Taxable Return Taxable Or Tax-Favored Tax-Favored
Why are you investing?	☐ Retirement ☐ For 10 years plus ☐ Sending child to college ☐ Purchase in 5 years ☐ Purchase in 3 years ☐ Purchase 3 years or less	Long To Very Long Long Intermediate To Long Intermediate Intermediate To Short Short Term
Do you have savings dedicated as emergency funds?	☐ 20% of income or less ☐ 40% of income or less ☐ 60% of income or more	Short Term Intermediate Long
Have you thoroughly reviewed your basic family protection plans and purchased adequate insurance?	☐ No ☐ Yes	Do not invest. Your basic insurance needs are the foundation on which a solid financial plan is built. Match the above responses to the investment selector grid on pages A10-A11.

INVESTMENT SELECTOR GRID	High Safety	Moderate Safety	Low Safety	Long-Term	Intermediate-Term	Short Term	Tax-Favored	Taxable	Income	Growth 10% or Better
Fixed Interest Investments:										
CD	X					X		X	X	
Government Securities	X					X		X	X	
Fixed Annuity	X			X			X	X	X	
Corporate Bonds		X		X				X		
Municipal Bonds		X			X		X		X	
Zero Coupon Bonds		X		X				X		
Mutual Funds:										
Utility Fund		X		X	X			X		X
Stock Index Fund		X	X	X	X			X		X
Conservative Stock Fund		X	X	X	X			X		X

General Quality Bond Fund	X	X		X	X			X	X	
GNMA Fund		X		X	X			X	X	
High Yield Bond Fund			X	X				X	X	X
Global Stock Fund			X	X				X		X
Option Growth Fund			X	X	X			X		X

The above classification will help you match your risk tolerance and goals with specific categories of investments. Please note that the above is generally true, but a specific offering may not exactly match. Before making any investment, always read the prospectus and evaluate your risk tolerance, holding period and the erosion effect.

Use the following investment checklist to specify the current value of each account. Next to the account value, enter in the change you would like to make to your plan.

Investment Checklist

Investment	Value of Account	Percent Increase	Percent Decrease	No Change
Checking Accounts				
Savings Accounts				
Certificates of Deposit				
Money Market Accounts				
Treasury Bills and Notes				
Life Insurance Cash Values				
Guaranteed Annuities				
Home Equity				
Bond Mutual Funds				
Stock Mutual Funds				
Variable Annuities				
Individual Bonds				
Individual Stocks				
Real Estate				
Precious Metals				
Venture Capital				
Stock Options				
Commodities				
Collectibles				
Other				
Other				

Retirement Calculation

1. Determine the percent of your current income you will need.

$\underline{\hspace{3cm}}$ x $\underline{\hspace{1.5cm}}$% = $\underline{\hspace{4cm}}$
(current income) (e.g., 70%)   (income needed)

2. Project your income from other sources at retirement.

Estimate annual pension benefits (your pension administrator at work can help you with this estimate):

$\underline{\hspace{3cm}}$

Estimate annual Social Security income (this information is on your Social Security verification form, see page 73): $\underline{\hspace{3cm}}$

Retirement savings to date: $\underline{\hspace{3cm}}$

3. Adjust numbers from 1 and 2 to accurately reflect the impact of 5% inflation.

Years to retirement	10	15	20	25
Inflation factors (5%)	1.63	2.08	2.65	3.39

$\underline{\hspace{3cm}}$ x $\underline{\hspace{1.5cm}}$ = $\underline{\hspace{4cm}}$
(income needed)   (factor)   (adjusted income needed)

$\underline{\hspace{3cm}}$ x $\underline{\hspace{1.5cm}}$ = $\underline{\hspace{4cm}}$
(pension)   (factor)   (adjusted pension)

$\underline{\hspace{3cm}}$ x $\underline{\hspace{1.5cm}}$ = $\underline{\hspace{4cm}}$
(Social Security) (factor)   (adjusted Social Security)

4. Subtract the adjusted pension and adjusted Social Security from the adjusted income needed.

$\underline{\hspace{3cm}}$ - $\underline{\hspace{3cm}}$ = $\underline{\hspace{4cm}}$
(adjusted income   (adjusted pension   (annual shortfall)
needed)   and adjusted
                    Social Security)

Annual shortfall divided by 12 = $\underline{\hspace{3cm}}$
(monthly shortfall)

5. The following table illustrates how much you will need in order to generate $100 in income for various lengths of time.

Years in retirement	Annual rate of return		
	8%	10%	12%
10 years	$8,397	$7,767	$7,213
15 years	$10,711	$9,614	$8,695
20 years	$12,286	$10,762	$9,536
25 years	$13,358	$11,474	$10,013

$_____ x $_____ = $_____
(amount from table)   (shortfall divided by 100)   (preliminary goal)

Example: Assume if your monthly shortfall is $2,000 and you want income to continue for 20 years. You anticipate a 10% rate of return. The intersection of 20 years and 10% is $10,762. Multiply $10,762 by 20 (your shortfall divided by 100). Your preliminary retirement goal equals $215,240.

6. The preliminary goal must be increased to account for inflation. A factor of 1.5 (conservative) to 2.0 (very conservative) will provide you with a rough estimate.

$_____ x _____ = $_____
(preliminary goal)   (factor 1.5 to 2.0)   (retirement goal)

7. The next step is to adjust current savings for the growth that you expect to occur between now and the day you retire.

Years to retirement	Annual rate of return		
	8%	10%	12%
10 years	2.16	2.59	3.11
15 years	3.17	4.18	5.47
20 years	4.66	6.73	9.65
25 years	6.85	10.83	17.00

$_____ x _____ = $_____
(current savings)   (factor)   (projected savings)

8. Determine your retirement gap by subtracting from your retirement goal the projected value of your savings calculated in step seven. A negative number means you are already in position to attain your goal.

$_____ - $_____ = $_____
(retirement goal)   (projected savings)   (retirement gap)

A-13

9. Now that you know what you will need, calculate how much you need to save each year to fill the gap.

Years to retirement	Annual rate of return		
	8%	10%	12%
10 years	.0690	.0627	.0570
15 years	.0368	.0315	.0268
20 years	.0219	.0175	.0139
25 years	.0137	.0102	.0075

$_____ x _____ = $_____
(retirement gap)   (factor)   (annual savings needed)

Divide your annual savings needed by 12 to determine the amount each month you need to save.

$_____ divided by 12 = $_____
(annual amount)   (monthly savings needed)

Could your financial plan benefit from a qualfied plan?

☐ Yes, I need to pursue implementing a qualfied retirement plan.

☐ No, I have adequate funds in qualified plans. I need to pursue implementing a non-qualified retirement plan.

☐ No, I am not concerned about retirement planning.

Does your financial plan need annuities?

☐ I need to investigate the power of annuities. I am confident that taxes will remain close to where they are today. Furthermore, I am not likely to incur the 10% penalty tax for distributions prior to age 59½.

☐ I have carefully reviewed the advantages of an annuity and am confident that my financial plan is better positioned without an annuity.

Do you need help implementing your plan?

☐ Yes, I need to consult with a financial professional (see chapter 10).

☐ No, I have already taken the necessary steps to implement my plan.

<u>Notes - Things to ask your financial consultant.</u>

_____

_____

_____

_____

_____

_____

_____

_____

_____

_____

_____

_____

_____

_____

_____

_____

_____

_____

_____

Congratulations on completing your financial plan.

Single Deposit Table

How much will $1,000 grow to in 10 years at 7% interest?

The answer is $1,970 ($1,000 x 1.97 = $1,970). The factor of 1.97 is found on the table below at the intersection of 7% and 10 years.

If you could earn 8% and wanted to accumulate $100,000 in 20 years, how much would you have to invest today?

The answer is $21,459.23 ($100,000 ÷ 4.66 = $21,459.23). The factor 4.66 is found on the table below at the intersection of 8% and 20 years.

End of Year	4%	5%	6%	7%	8%	9%	10%	11%	12%	13%	14%
1	1.04	1.05	1.06	1.07	1.08	1.09	1.10	1.11	1.12	1.13	1.14
2	1.08	1.10	1.12	1.14	1.17	1.19	1.21	1.23	1.25	1.28	1.30
3	1.12	1.16	1.19	1.23	1.26	1.30	1.33	1.37	1.40	1.44	1.48
4	1.17	1.22	1.26	1.31	1.36	1.41	1.46	1.52	1.57	1.63	1.69
5	1.22	1.28	1.34	1.40	1.47	1.54	1.61	1.69	1.76	1.84	1.93
6	1.27	1.34	1.42	1.50	1.59	1.68	1.77	1.87	1.97	2.08	2.19
7	1.32	1.41	1.50	1.61	1.71	1.83	1.95	2.08	2.21	2.35	2.50
8	1.37	1.48	1.59	1.72	1.85	1.99	2.14	2.30	2.48	2.66	2.85
9	1.42	1.55	1.69	1.84	2.00	2.17	2.36	2.56	2.77	3.00	3.25
10	1.48	1.63	1.79	1.97	2.16	2.37	2.59	2.84	3.11	3.39	3.71
11	1.54	1.71	1.90	2.10	2.33	2.58	2.85	3.15	3.48	3.84	4.23
12	1.60	1.80	2.01	2.25	2.52	2.81	3.14	3.50	3.90	4.33	4.82
13	1.67	1.89	2.13	2.41	2.72	3.07	3.45	3.88	4.36	4.90	5.49
14	1.73	1.98	2.26	2.58	2.94	3.34	3.80	4.31	4.89	5.53	6.26
15	1.80	2.08	2.40	2.76	3.17	3.64	4.18	4.78	5.47	6.25	7.14
16	1.87	2.18	2.54	2.95	3.43	3.97	4.59	5.31	6.13	7.07	8.14
17	1.95	2.29	2.69	3.16	3.70	4.33	5.05	5.90	6.87	7.99	9.28
18	2.03	2.41	2.85	3.38	4.00	4.72	5.56	6.54	7.69	9.02	10.58
19	2.11	2.53	3.03	3.62	4.32	5.14	6.12	7.26	8.61	10.20	12.06
20	2.19	2.65	3.21	3.87	4.66	5.60	6.73	8.06	9.65	11.52	13.74
21	2.28	2.79	3.40	4.14	5.03	6.11	7.40	8.95	10.80	13.02	15.67
22	2.37	2.93	3.60	4.43	5.44	6.66	8.14	9.93	12.10	14.71	17.86
23	2.46	3.07	3.82	4.74	5.87	7.26	8.95	11.03	13.55	16.63	20.36
24	2.56	3.23	4.05	5.07	6.34	7.91	9.85	12.24	15.18	18.79	23.21
25	2.67	3.39	4.29	5.43	6.85	8.62	10.83	13.59	17.00	21.23	26.46
26	2.77	3.56	4.55	5.81	7.40	9.40	11.92	15.08	19.04	23.99	30.17
27	2.88	3.73	4.82	6.21	7.99	10.25	13.11	16.74	21.32	27.11	34.39
28	3.00	3.92	5.11	6.65	8.63	11.17	14.42	18.58	23.88	30.63	39.20
29	3.12	4.12	5.42	7.11	9.32	12.17	15.86	20.62	26.75	34.62	44.69
30	3.24	4.32	5.74	7.61	10.06	13.27	17.45	22.89	29.96	39.12	50.95
31	3.37	4.54	6.09	8.15	10.87	14.46	19.19	25.41	33.56	44.20	58.08
32	3.51	4.76	6.45	8.72	11.74	15.76	21.11	28.21	37.58	49.95	66.21
33	3.65	5.00	6.84	9.33	12.68	17.18	23.23	31.31	42.09	56.44	75.48
34	3.79	5.25	7.25	9.98	13.69	18.73	25.55	34.75	47.14	63.78	86.05
35	3.95	5.52	7.69	10.68	14.79	20.41	28.10	38.57	52.80	72.07	98.10
36	4.10	5.79	8.15	11.42	15.97	22.25	30.91	42.82	59.14	81.44	111.83
37	4.27	6.08	8.64	12.22	17.25	24.25	34.00	47.53	66.23	92.02	127.49
38	4.44	6.39	9.15	13.08	18.63	26.44	37.40	52.76	74.18	103.99	145.34
39	4.62	6.70	9.70	13.99	20.12	28.82	41.14	58.56	83.08	117.51	165.69
40	4.80	7.04	10.29	14.97	21.72	31.41	45.26	65.00	93.05	132.78	188.88

Constant Deposit Table

How much will $1,000 per year grow to in 10 years at 7% interest?

The answer is $14,780 ($1,000 x 14.78 = $14,780). The factor of 14.78 is found on the table below at the intersection of 10 years and 7%.

How much would have to be put away each year at 8% interest in order to accumulate $1,000,000 in 40 years?

The answer is $3,574.24 ($1,000,000 ÷ 279.78 = $3,574.24). The factor of 279.78 is found on the table below at the intersection of 8% and 40 years.

End of Year	4%	5%	6%	7%	8%	9%	10%	11%	12%	13%	14%
1	1.04	1.05	1.06	1.07	1.08	1.09	1.10	1.11	1.12	1.13	1.14
2	2.12	2.15	2.18	2.21	2.25	2.28	2.31	2.34	2.37	2.41	2.44
3	3.25	3.31	3.37	3.44	3.51	3.57	3.64	3.71	3.78	3.85	3.92
4	4.42	4.53	4.64	4.75	4.87	4.98	5.11	5.23	5.35	5.48	5.61
5	5.63	5.80	5.98	6.15	6.34	6.52	6.72	6.91	7.12	7.32	7.54
6	6.90	7.14	7.39	7.65	7.92	8.20	8.49	8.78	9.09	9.40	9.73
7	8.21	8.55	8.90	9.26	9.64	10.03	10.44	10.86	11.30	11.76	12.23
8	9.58	10.03	10.49	10.98	11.49	12.02	12.58	13.16	13.78	14.42	15.09
9	11.01	11.58	12.18	12.82	13.49	14.19	14.94	15.72	16.55	17.42	18.34
10	12.49	13.21	13.97	**14.78**	15.65	16.56	17.53	18.56	19.65	20.81	22.04
11	14.03	14.92	15.87	16.89	17.98	19.14	20.38	21.71	23.13	24.65	26.27
12	15.63	16.71	17.88	19.14	20.50	21.95	23.52	25.21	27.03	28.98	31.09
13	17.29	18.60	20.02	21.55	23.21	25.02	26.97	29.09	31.39	33.88	36.58
14	19.02	20.58	22.28	24.13	26.15	28.36	30.77	33.41	36.28	39.42	42.84
15	20.82	22.66	24.67	26.89	29.32	32.00	34.95	38.19	41.75	45.67	49.98
16	22.70	24.84	27.21	29.84	32.75	35.97	39.54	43.50	47.88	52.74	58.12
17	24.65	27.31	29.91	33.00	36.45	40.30	44.60	49.40	54.75	60.73	67.36
18	26.67	29.54	32.76	36.38	40.45	45.02	50.16	55.94	62.44	69.75	77.96
19	28.78	32.07	35.79	40.00	46.76	50.16	56.27	63.20	71.02	79.95	90.02
20	30.97	34.72	38.99	43.87	49.42	55.76	63.00	71.27	80.70	91.47	103.77
21	33.25	37.51	42.39	48.01	54.46	61.87	70.40	80.21	91.50	104.49	119.44
22	35.62	40.43	46.00	52.44	59.89	68.53	78.54	90.15	103.60	119.20	137.30
23	38.08	43.50	49.82	57.18	65.76	75.79	87.50	101.17	117.16	135.83	157.66
24	40.65	46.73	53.86	62.25	72.11	83.70	97.35	113.41	132.33	154.62	180.87
25	43.31	50.11	58.16	67.68	78.95	92.32	108.18	127.00	149.33	175.85	207.33
26	46.08	53.67	62.71	73.48	86.35	101.72	120.10	142.08	168.37	199.84	237.50
27	48.97	57.40	67.53	79.70	94.34	111.97	133.31	158.82	189.70	226.95	271.89
28	51.97	61.32	72.64	86.35	102.97	123.14	147.63	177.40	213.58	257.54	311.09
29	55.08	65.44	78.06	93.46	112.28	135.31	163.49	198.02	240.33	292.20	355.79
30	58.33	69.76	83.80	101.07	122.35	148.58	180.94	220.91	270.29	331.32	406.74
31	61.70	74.30	89.89	109.22	133.21	163.04	200.14	246.32	303.85	375.52	464.82
32	65.21	79.06	96.34	117.93	144.95	178.80	221.25	274.53	341.43	425.46	531.04
33	68.86	84.07	103.18	127.26	157.63	195.98	244.48	305.84	383.52	481.90	606.52
34	72.65	89.32	110.43	137.24	171.32	214.71	270.02	340.59	430.66	545.68	692.57
35	76.60	94.84	118.12	147.91	186.10	235.12	298.13	379.16	483.46	616.75	790.67
36	80.70	100.63	126.27	159.34	202.07	257.38	329.04	421.98	542.60	699.19	902.51
37	84.97	106.71	134.90	171.56	219.32	281.63	363.04	469.51	608.83	791.21	1030.00
38	89.41	113.10	144.06	184.64	237.94	308.07	400.45	522.27	683.01	895.20	1175.34
39	94.03	119.80	153.76	198.64	258.06	336.88	441.59	580.83	766.09	1012.70	1341.03
40	98.83	126.84	164.05	213.61	**279.78**	368.29	486.85	645.83	859.14	1145.49	1529.91

Index

----------------------- *A* --------------------

Accelerated benefits, 32-33, 40
A.M. Best, 86
Annuities, 79-81
Assets, 12
Asset inventory, 16
Asset protection, 5, 22
Automobile insurance, 44-45

----------------------- *B* --------------------

Banking system, 10
Bankruptcy, 21
Bonds, 53-54
Budgeting, 12

----------------------- *C* --------------------

Car loans, 18
Cash flow, 12
Certificates of deposit, 51
Certified Financial Planners, 25
Changes, 15
Chartered Financial Consultants, 25,
    84
Chartered Life Underwriters, 84
Choosing a financial service
    company, 83, 85-87
COBRA, 46
Collectibles, 55
College funding, 67-70
Commodities, 55
Common stocks, 53
Consumer credit counseling
    services, 21
Contingency day, 11
Convenient time to save, 6
Corporate bonds, 54
Cost of college, 67-68, 70
Credit cards, 17-18
Creditor proofing assets, 22, 35, 74

----------------------- *D* --------------------

Debt management, 17-21
Debt ratio, 19-20
Disability income insurance, 4-5,
    42-44, 70
Discipline, 17
Dollar cost averaging, 57-59
Dow Jones Industrial Average, 49-50
Drowning in debt, 21

----------------------- *E* --------------------

Education planning, 67-70
Emergency access, 5, 11, 62, 70

Equities, 53
Erosion effect, 49-52
Estate planning, 26-28
Estate taxes, 9, 26-28

----------------------- *F* --------------------

Federal Deposit Insurance
Corporation, 10
Federal Estate Tax, 9, 26-28
Financial consultants, 25, 82
Financial organization, 11-12
Financial product hierarchy, 13
Financial professionals, 15, 83-87
Financial roller coaster, 1
Financial trap, 17
Future:
    future shock in action, 3
    self-ppraisal, 10
    taxes, 7-9

----------------------- *G* --------------------

Goals, 12-15
Gold, 55
Government securities, 54
Grandfathering, 9

----------------------- *H* --------------------

Health care, 8, 45-46
Home equity loan, 19, 69
Homeowners insurance, 45

----------------------- *I* --------------------

Ibbotson & Associates:
    historical performance chart, 32,
    60
Income taxes:
    brackets, 23-24
    exemptions, 24
    future considerations, 7-9
    standard deduction, 24
    strategies, 25-26
    tables, 23-24, 26
Individual Retirement Accounts, 75-
    76
Inflation, 41-42, 51
Insurance:
    accelerated benefits, 32-33, 40
    accidental death, 47
    consumer purchase, 48
    credit card, 47
    disability, 5, 42-44, 70
    dread disease, 48

i

flight, 47
health, 45-46
life, 5, 29-42
long term care, 46
medical, 45-46
medicare, 46
option to purchase additional, 48
property & casualty, 44-45
student, 48
umbrella, 22
Investments:
    alternatives, 52-56
    annuities, 67-69
    certificates of deposit, 51
    checklist for, 56-57
    collectibles, 55
    commodities, 55
    common stock, 53
    corporate bonds, 54
    diversification, 53
    dollar cost averaging, 57-59
    equities, 53
    government securities, 54
    historic performance (Ibbotson),
    32, 60
    impact of inflation, 41-42, 51
    municipal bonds, 54
    mutual funds, 53
    precious stones, 55
    predicting the market, 59-60
    preferred stock, 53
    real estate, 54
    risk, 49-50, 52
    selector, 52
    Series EE and HH bonds, 53-54
    stable growth wins, 60
    stock options, 55
    time horizon, 5, 50
    venture capital, 54

---------------------- L --------------------

Legal documents, 16
Legal reserve system, 81
Liabilities, 12
Life expectancies, 10, 61
Life insurance:
    accelerated benefits, 32-33, 40
    calculating your need, 40-41
    history, 29, 31
    inflation, 41-42
    mechanics, 33-40
    option to purchase additional, 48
    tax advantages, 29-40, 63-66, 76-
    79
    term, 29-31, 34

whole life, 29-31, 34-35
universal, 29-31, 35
variable, 29-31, 35-41
Living trust, 16
Long term care, 46

--------------------- M --------------------

Market timing, 59
Medical insurance, 45-46
Medicare, 46
Mortality curve, 33
Mortality table, 30
Mortgage acceleration, 61-66
Municipal bonds, 54
Mutual funds, 53

---------------------- N --------------------

National debt, 7
Nationalized health care, 8
Net worth, 12

--------------------- O --------------------

Organization:
    cash flow, 12
    contingency planning, 11
    financial professionals, 15
    goals, 12-15
    net worth, 12
    videotaping valuables, 16
    wills, 16

--------------------- P --------------------

PE ratio, 59
Pensions,
    defined benefit, 64-65
    defined contribution, 37-40, 64-65
Personal asset inventory, 16
Personal catastrophe liability, 22
Post-retirement, 81-82
Pre-retirement, 71
Precious stones, 55
Preferred stock, 53
Price earnings ratio, 59
Prioritizing goals, 13-14
Private pension plan:
    benefits, 76-79
    comparison, 36-40, 77
    questions and answers, 78
Procrastination:
    get started, 4
    theater fire, 17

Property and casualty insurance, 44-
    45

---------------------- Q --------------------

Qualifying for credit, 18
Qualified retirement plans, 37-40, 74-75

---------------------- R --------------------

Real estate, 54
Retirement planning:
　　100 person story, 2
　　annuities, 79-81
　　calculating need, 71-73
　　component of six perspectives, 5
　　hidden risk in pension plans, 74-75
　　hidden risk in annuities, 81
　　individual retirement accounts, 75-76
　　individual plans, 75-82
　　individual savings, 2
　　post-retirement planning, 81-82
　　pre-retirement planning, 71
　　private pension plan, 39, 76-79, 82
　　qualified pension plans, 8-9, 37-40, 74-75
　　simplified employee pension plans, 64
　　Social Security, 2, 7-8, 73
　　three legs of retirement income, 63
Risk, 49-50, 52
Rule of 72, 4

---------------------- S --------------------

Saving to spend, 2
Secret to success, 1, 60
Section 1035 exchange, 83
Series EE and HH bonds, 53-54
Setting goals, 14
Simplified employee pension plans, 64
Six perspectives of financial planning, 4-5, 68-70
Social Security:
　　9 digits enough, 7
　　demographic projections, 2,7
　　disability benefits, 73-74
　　retirement benefits, 7-8, 73-74
　　survivor benefits, 73
　　tax on Social Security income, 9
　　verifying benefits, 73-74
Sound principles, 5, 69
Snapshots in time, 6
Stock market, 49-60

---------------------- T --------------------

Taxes:
　　calculating your taxes, 23-24
　　deferral formula, 52
　　estate, 9, 26-28
　　future, 7-8
　　income, 8, 23-24
　　reduction strategies, 25-26
　　Section 1035 exchange, 85
　　transfer tax, 26
　　trends, 8-9
Term life insurance, 29-31, 34
Trusts, 16, 22

---------------------- U --------------------

Unconventional phases in life, 10
Universal life insurance, 29-31, 35

-------------------- V to Z --------------------

Variable life insurance, 29-31, 35-41
Venture capital, 54
Wealth organization, 11-16
Wills, 16
Whole life insurance, 29-31, 34-40